THE ULTIMATE VEGETARIAN
SLOW COOKER COOKBOOK

THE ULTIMATE
Vegetarian
SLOW COOKER
COOKBOOK

200 FLAVORFUL AND FILLING MEATLESS
RECIPES THAT PREP FAST AND COOK SLOW

Linda Larsen

SONOMA
PRESS

Photography © 2016 Stocksy/Davide Illini, Cover; Stocksy/Sarah Lalone, p.2; Stocksy/J.R. PHOTOGRAPHY, p.6; Stockfood/Gräfe & Unzer Verlag / Jörn Rynio, p.8; Stocksy/Ina Peters, p.22; Stockfood/Eva Gründemann, p.30; Stocksy/Jeff Wasserman, p.40; Stockfood/Gräfe & Unzer Verlag/Jörn Rynio, p.48; Stockfood/Veslemøy Vråskar, p.58; Stocksy/Harald Walker, p.76; Stocksy/Harald Walker, p.100; Stocksy/Ina Peters, p.104; Stocksy/Nataša Mandić, p.116; Stockfood/Jacqui Blanchard Photography, p.126; Stockfood/Jim Norton, p.132; Stockfood/Meike Bergmann, p.152; Stockfood/James Franco, p.158; Stocksy/Davide Illini, p.170; Stocksy/Nataša Mandić, p.182; Stocksy/Pixel Stories, p.188; Stocksy/Ali Harper, p.192; Stocksy/Harald Walker, p.206; Stocksy/Ina Peters, p.212; Stockfood/Eising Studio - Food Photo & Video, p.224; Stocksy/Sara Remington, p.244; Stocksy/Jeff Wasserman, p.254; Stocksy/Davide Illini, p.268.

ISBN: Print 978-1-943451-42-5 | eBook 978-1-943451-43-2

CONTENTS

Are you interested in adding vegetarian recipes to your repertoire? You may be intrigued, but concerned that meals made without meat are bland, uninteresting, and difficult to make. Not true! Vegetarian dishes can be flavorful and bright, with lots of wonderful and delicious flavors and pleasing textures, and making these recipes in the slow cooker makes cooking very easy on you.

Whether you want to follow the "Meatless Monday" trend, cut down on your meat consumption because you're concerned about sustainability and the environment, or just want to try something new, these recipes will introduce you into a new and different lifestyle. I am not a vegetarian, but I go meatless a few times a week—and I don't miss the meat one bit. The recipes in this book are delicious, and you won't miss the meat either. Not only are they hearty, satisfying, and healthy, they are varied and interesting. And it doesn't hurt that they're easier on your wallet.

Many vegetarian recipes are built on ingredients such as beans and root vegetables, and the slow cooker is the perfect way to cook them. This wonderful appliance transforms these humble ingredients into some spectacularly flavorful meals. You can make delicious vegetarian recipes that range from an Indian curry to a Tex-Mex feast to classic American comfort foods in the slow cooker. The slow cooker works its magic while you get on with your busy life. You can throw food in the ceramic insert, turn the slow cooker on, go to work or school or run errands all day, and come home to a delicious meal that's waiting for you.

These recipes rely on good fats from nuts and seeds, and they're packed full of nutrients from the many different beans, leafy greens, and vegetables available in the market. So get your slow cooker ready, and dive in. These delicious recipes are easy to make and satisfying.

BEYOND BROCCOLI

CHAPTER ONE

VEGETARIAN FOOD has a reputation for being difficult or time-consuming to make. While that may have been true back when we had to shell beans and peas and make our own tofu, most grocery stores have lots of slow cooker-ready whole foods and minimally processed foods that make vegetarian cooking a breeze.

And forget about the rumor that vegetarian meals are flavorless. Nothing could be farther from the truth. With the addition of herbs and spices, along with naturally flavorful vegetables and greens, these meals pop with flavor. The slow cooker is a sealed cooking appliance, which means that more flavor is kept in the pot. Long, slow, moist cooking makes root vegetables tender and turns hard lentils and dried beans into silky, delicious, satisfying mouthfuls.

In this chapter, we'll cover the tips and techniques you need to know to make all of your vegetarian slow cooker meals delicious and very easy. Let's get started!

GO-TO GROCERIES

The grocery store is a treasure trove for vegetarian cooks. Fresh, frozen, dried, canned—ingredient options for the slow cooker are many and varied. If you typically skip the bulk aisle, here's your chance to take advantage of it. The myriad beans and lentils and other great products are perfect for the slow cooker. These foods are the staples and basics of vegetarian cooking, so shop and stock up.

Note: In cooking instructions, sorting dried beans, peas, or lentils means looking through them and removing and discarding any inedible material, such as small twigs, stones, or dirt clumps.

SLOW COOKER SIZES

Slow cookers range from a tiny 4-cup model to behemoths that hold 7 quarts. Most recipes in this book are for 4- or 5-quart slow cookers that hold 16 to 20 cups of ingredients. But if you have a slow cooker that's a different size, don't worry. To adjust the recipes to your size of slow cooker, simply increase or decrease the amount of solids and liquids. For instance, if you have a 3-quart slow cooker and want to make a recipe developed for a 4-quart model, reduce all of the ingredients by 25 percent. If the recipe calls for 6 cups of vegetable broth and 6 cups of vegetables, use 4½ cups of broth and 4½ cups of vegetables. Just make sure the slow cooker is filled ¾ full in order for the food to cook properly. The same goes if you have a larger slow cooker. If you have a 6-quart model, increase the food and liquid for a recipe that cooks in a 4-quart slow cooker by 25 percent. The nice thing about savory slow cooker recipes is that, unlike baking recipes, they are quite adaptable—add a little extra or a little less of an ingredient, and the results are equally delicious. That means you can make changes, and the recipe will still work.

Lentils

BROWN The most common type of lentil, these little rounds are delicious in soups. They become mushy when overcooked and may lose their shape, but that helps them thicken soups and stews. Brown lentils have a mild flavor and velvety texture. They are the least expensive type of lentil and are readily available.

RED These brightly colored legumes are a great addition to many recipes. They also become soft when overcooked and can lose their shape. They cook quickly because they are usually sold split, which make them ideal for soups, chowders, and stews. Red lentils are commonly used in South Asian recipes.

GREEN Green lentils usually take the longest to cook. They stay firm but tender after cooking and hold their shape well, so they are perfect for salads and side dishes. Green lentils have a slightly peppery flavor and mix well with spicy ingredients such as curry powder, red chiles, and oregano.

FRENCH French lentils, also called Le Puy lentils because they are grown in that region of France, hold their shape very well once cooked, so they are wonderful in salads and casseroles. These tiny dark green legumes also have a peppery and slightly earthy flavor. French lentils are considered the best for slow cooking and are the most expensive of the lentil options.

BLACK Black lentils, also called beluga lentils since they resemble caviar, are higher in protein than other lentil varieties. They are native to Syria. These very small legumes have a soft texture when cooked and a mild, earthy flavor. They are a great addition to soups or casseroles.

MUNG Mung lentils, also called mung dal, are actually mung beans that have the skins removed and are split in half. This type of lentil cooks very quickly and becomes quite soft in the slow cooker. They are good to use for thickening soups and stews since they almost dissolve in the long, slow cooking process.

Beans

PINTO The Spanish word *pinto* means "painted," and like the horse of the same name, dry pinto beans are beige with brown spots. When cooked, they have a smooth pink appearance. These beans are quite high in protein and have a creamy texture. Typically associated with refried beans, they are delicious in soups and chili, too.

BLACK Also called turtle beans, black beans have a shiny black coat and are a creamy white color inside once cooked. Black beans are very high in antioxidants that may help prevent cancer, and they're delicious! The beans keep their shape nicely after cooking and have a wonderful velvety texture.

CHICKPEA Chickpeas are also called garbanzo beans. You can buy them dry, but they are most often sold canned. These beans are very high in fiber, which according to pharmacist Jennifer Moll helps regulate blood choles- terol levels. They are used to make hummus and are wonderful in soups and on salads.

KIDNEY These beans can be a deep pink color or a white color. The white kidney beans are also known as cannellini beans. Either type of bean is available dried or canned. They are used most often in soups and chili. Kidney beans are high in fiber and help stabilize blood sugar.

GREAT NORTHERN Great Northern beans are white, with a slightly tougher skin than other bean varieties, and have a nutty flavor. A good substitute for them is navy beans, which are smaller and a little sweeter. Both types of beans are good in soup; in fact, the Great Northern is sometimes called the "soup bean."

Crucifers

BRUSSELS SPROUTS These may look like little cabbages, but they aren't. They are part of the same family, though. When properly prepared, they can be tender and sweet. The slow cooker gives them slightly crisp and browned edges when they are cooked with butter and ingredients such as mustard, maple syrup, or brown sugar. This technique has converted many a formerly confirmed Brussels sprouts hater.

CAULIFLOWER Cauliflower is such a healthy food, and it cooks so well in your slow cooker. It is full of antioxidants that help prevent cancer and reduce inflammation. You can find white, green, purple, and orange varieties of cauliflower on the market. All are mild in flavor with a tender texture when cooked.

BROCCOLI Broccoli is another nutrition powerhouse, with lots of antioxidants, plus vitamins A and C. It's best cooked in the slow cooker for only a short time so it retains a crisp-tender texture. Add it to soups and stews at the end of the cooking time for best results. It's also delicious in soups when cooked until soft and puréed.

CABBAGES There are so many colors and types of cabbage, and it's so affordable! You can find white (or green) cabbage, red (or purple) cabbage, savoy, and napa. They all cook beautifully in the slow cooker and turn silky and sweet. Cabbage is also full of antioxidants and fiber and is very healthy.

BOK CHOY This is a type of Chinese cabbage that looks more like celery, but the two are not related. It is packed with vitamin A and fiber. It tastes a little bitter when raw, but that taste mellows when the cabbage is cooked. It is used often in stir-fries, but it's also tailor-made for the slow cooker.

Tubers

POTATOES Just about everyone loves potatoes! You can find so many types of potatoes on the market: the standard russet, buttery Yukon Gold, smaller creamer potatoes, tiny red potatoes, purple, white, and fingerling. They are a good source of vitamins B_6 and C, niacin, and fiber. They all cook beautifully in the slow cooker.

SWEET POTATOES Sweet potatoes are not yams, and yams are not sweet potatoes; they are two different plant roots. The type you see in the store is a sweet potato (even if it's called a yam), and it has a dense orange flesh. This root vegetable is a slow cooker staple. It turns velvety smooth and extremely sweet when cooked for a long time.

BEETS Preparing beets in the slow cooker is a great way to introduce them to anyone reluctant about trying them. Sweet, silky, and tender, they are a

perfect vegetable for the slow cooker. Beets are a good source of folate, fiber, vitamin C, and iron, and they are very inexpensive. Delicious and healthy, they should be part of your diet.

TURNIPS These may be considered an "old-fashioned" vegetable, but they are very inexpensive and good for you—not to mention delicious and great for the slow cooker. Turnips have a purple and white skin and a slightly peppery flavor. They are delicious in soups and stews and make an excellent substitute for mashed potatoes when cooked until tender and mashed with butter.

CELERY ROOT This big, lumpy-looking root has a mild celery flavor—what a surprise! This is not the root of a celery plant but a special plant cultivated just for the root. It is certainly not the most attractive root vegetable out there, but once trimmed it's delicious raw or cooked. This vegetable makes a wonderful soup or salad.

Leafy Greens

KALE Kale burst into the mainstream culinary scene a few years ago, and many people love it—and with good reason. It is one of the healthiest foods you can eat; it can lower the risk of many different kinds of cancer, and it lowers cholesterol, too, according to *Authority Nutrition*. This leafy green is good raw but even better cooked, when it becomes soft and mild.

SPINACH Everyone has had spinach; it's a childhood staple, even though many kids don't like it. When cooked in the slow cooker, it is very mild and sweet. It's good in soups and vegetable dishes and a real star in layered casseroles such as lasagna. Spinach is high in vitamin C and carotenoids, antioxidants that reduce inflammation.

ESCAROLE This green is a type of endive that has a bitter taste. It is high in vitamins A and K, and folic acid. The outermost dark greens are best for cooking and are perfect for soups made in the slow cooker. Choose firm heads with vibrant color and smooth leaves.

ARUGULA Also known as rocket, this leafy green vegetable is an annual herb. It belongs to the same Brassica family as cauliflower and kale. In cooking, arugula is usually eaten raw, but it is added to soups and stews at the end of cooking time to provide a vibrant note of color and peppery flavor.

Toothsome Twists

TOFU This vegetarian staple is made from soybeans. It comes in several textures, ranging from a very soft type used in puddings to a firm tofu that can actually be cooked on the grill. It makes a wonderful curry or chili, and provides complete protein when combined with grains or seeds.

TEMPEH Like tofu, tempeh is made from fermented soybeans, but offers a different texture. It is sold in flat rectangles and is a light brown color. You can usually see the soybeans in the tempeh. The consistency is firm and chewy with a slightly sweet taste. It has more fiber and protein than tofu. It can be crumbled and added to casseroles, pasta sauces, and soups.

GROUND BEEF SUBSTITUTES Usually sold refrigerated, these hearty crumbles are a satisfying addition to your repertoire. Generally made of soy and wheat, the crumbles look and taste remarkably like cooked ground beef. They cook beautifully in the slow cooker and are especially good in chili. It's important to read the label of any processed food you buy and make sure that you are not allergic to anything on the ingredient list.

Tasty Toppings

HOT SAUCE Hot sauce adds heat to any dish, and it should be used based on your preferred heat level. Its flavor diminishes when cooked for a long time, so add it at the end of slow cooking. Which to use? Everyone has their own personal favorite—I always have a big bottle of my favorite in the pantry.

SALSA Salsa can be hot or mild, made of vegetables, fruit, or even legumes. The hottest salsas have habanero chiles—look out for their signature orange color. Fruit salsas are a nice change of pace and can be a great garnish for stews and chili. You can easily make your own salsas with fresh seasonal ingredients, or there are many varieties available for purchase.

SOUR CREAM This smooth sauce adds body and a pleasant tartness. The casein in sour cream, as in all dairy, helps cool down spicy foods by binding capsaicin oils and removing them from your tongue. Add it as a topping or at the very last minute of cooking time so it doesn't separate.

FRESH VS. FROZEN VS. DRIED VS. CANNED

Why use dried when canned is available? Many ingredients are available in multiple forms. The chart below gives information and tips on common slow cooker vegetables, beans, and legumes in the different forms in which they are available.

	FRESH	FROZEN	DRIED	CANNED
Asparagus	Best fresh; add at the end of cooking time	Tends to be soft; add at the end of cooking time	Not available	Not recommended; texture is very soft
Broccoli	Cooks very well in the slow cooker	Good for the slow cooker; add at the end of cooking time	Not available	Not recommended
Cauliflower	Great in the slow cooker	Add at the end of cooking time	Not available	Not recommended
Green beans	Great in the slow cooker; remove the ends before cooking	Good added at the end of cooking time	Not available	Not recommended; texture is very soft
Herbs	Add soft herbs such as basil or oregano at the end of cooking time for a punch of bright flavor. Heartier herbs such as rosemary or thyme can be added at the beginning; remove the stems before serving	Not available	Great for the slow cooker; add at beginning of cooking time; you can add more at the end if necessary	Not available

	FRESH	FROZEN	DRIED	CANNED
Kale and Other Dark Greens	Cooks very well in the slow cooker	Good if added at the end of cooking time	Not available	Not recommended
Legumes or beans	You can sometimes find fresh, more often dried	Lima beans and edamame are good frozen	Dried beans are inexpensive, readily available, and good in the slow cooker	Canned beans are a convenience for soups and stews
Mushrooms	Readily available; cooks well in the slow cooker	Not available	Good way to buy more exotic types; work well in the slow cooker	Good for casseroles and soups
Onions	Great in the slow cooker; become tender and sweet	Tiny frozen pearl onions work very well in the slow cooker	Not recommended	Not recommended
Potatoes	Great in the slow cooker	Hash browns cook well in the slow cooker	Not recommended	Not recommended
Tomatoes	Great in the slow cooker	Not available	Add concentrated flavor to soups and stews	Good in stews and soups

RICE VINEGAR This light vinegar is made from fermented rice or rice wine. It has a mild, slightly sweet flavor. You can buy seasoned rice vinegar, but be aware that some brands contain corn syrup and monosodium glutamate (MSG). It is usually used in salad dressings and to make sushi rice, but it adds a delicate acidity that beautifully finishes slow cooker soups and stews, too.

SHREDDED CHEESE There are so many kinds of cheese available that you could spend weeks browsing through the selection in most stores. Cheese is

TO LINE OR NOT TO LINE

Once your delicious slow-cooked meal is ready, getting it out of the slow cooker can be tricky. You may want to line the cooker with a plastic liner, aluminum foil, or parchment paper, or you can simply spray the ceramic insert with nonstick cooking spray. There are disadvantages and advantages to all of these methods.

If you want to use a plastic liner, only use those specifically made for use in the slow cooker. Other plastic bags may melt in the insert and leach chemicals into your food. If you use a plastic liner, look for one that is labeled BPA-free. BPA is an endocrine disruptor used to make plastic flexible. Some people don't like cooking their food in plastic, but according to Reynolds, the BPA-free liners are approved by the FDA.

Foil liners are simple to use; you just tear off a few strips of foil and mold it into a liner. You should make sure the strips are long enough to extend outside the ceramic insert on either side. This way, you simply pull the foil up to remove the food. Parchment paper works the same way. This paper is heavy enough that it won't burn during cooking, but it may turn brown.

The simplest method is to spray the ceramic insert with nonstick cooking spray. The insert will be easy to clean, and you won't create more waste. The choice is yours.

the perfect topping for soups and stews and is a main component in lasagna and enchiladas. If you are going to melt the cheese in a sauce, shred the cheese yourself, as preshredded cheese doesn't melt as well.

CROUTONS Homemade croutons are so easy to make and add a lovely crunchy topping to slow cooked dishes. To make your own, just cube bread, drizzle it with extra-virgin olive oil, and bake in a 375°F oven until crunchy and brown, about 15 minutes. Store refrigerated in an airtight container.

LEMON JUICE Freshly squeezed lemon juice adds a bright pop of flavor to your dishes. Roll the lemon on the counter using the palm of your hand to get more juice out of each little yellow fruit. Bottled lemon juice doesn't have the fresh, strong taste of fresh, but it will do in a pinch.

PREP, PERFECTED

It's all in the preparation. A well-organized kitchen and a system for preparing ingredients for the slow cooker will save you time and let you get on with your day that much faster. These basic tips will help you make the most of your time in the kitchen, efficiently and expertly. Learn the best way to use a knife, set up your kitchen, save time with ingredients, and store foods for more efficient cooking.

Knife Skills

First make sure your knife is properly sharpened. Then grasp the handle in your dominant hand. Hold onto the handle with the last three fingers and use your forefinger and thumb to grasp the top of the base of the blade to keep the knife steady.

Hold the food with your other hand with your fingertips curled, so that if the blade accidentally slips, it will graze your nails instead of cutting your skin. Cut by placing the tip of the knife on the work surface, and moving the blade down through the food. Use the knuckles of the hand holding the food as a guide. To chop, turn the food 90 degrees and cut again. Chopped is the largest cut, followed by diced and then minced.

Kitchen Setup

Every kitchen is different, but each kitchen can be made as efficient as possible. The French term *mise en place* (rhymes with "peas on floss"), which means "put in place," suggests that you assemble your ingredients, utensils, and tools before you start cooking.

Make sure that you have an empty garbage can or trash bag nearby, or a container if you compost vegetable peelings. Some nonstick cooking spray or an oil mister is used for most recipes. Gather all of the ingredients together, and sort them according to the prep they will need before they go into the slow cooker. Then start working.

Time, Store-Bought

You can purchase some prepared ingredients to help cut down on your prep time. Boxed vegetable broth is a good option, as are some precut vegetables. You can find cauliflower and broccoli florets, sliced carrots, shredded carrots, sliced mushrooms, and peeled and chopped garlic in most grocery store produce aisles. Canned beans are a great time saver, as are jarred pasta sauces, prepared pesto, and roasted red peppers. Make sure that you taste these foods before you make them a regular item on your shopping list and that you and your family like them.

Super Easy Storage

If you make a lot of similar recipes in the slow cooker, get a head start on the week by preparing ingredients ahead of time. For instance, if you know you are going to make a lot of recipes using onions, chop five or six onions and store them in the refrigerator in a zipper-top bag. If you love cooking dried beans, soak a few bags of beans on Sunday night. Then drain them Monday morning and refrigerate, tightly covered, until you're ready to cook.

Leftovers should be promptly and properly refrigerated or frozen as soon as you are finished with the meal. Cover foods tightly, and label them so you'll know what you have stored. Dedicate a space in the refrigerator and freezer for leftovers so they don't get lost or spoiled.

USING YOUR SLOW COOKER: DOS AND DON'TS

The slow cooker is a pretty simple appliance. It consists of a metal surround that provides the heat, a ceramic insert that holds the food (which is usually removable for easy cleaning), and a lid that fits snugly onto the top of the insert. The lid provides a seal that holds in moisture. Some slow cookers have programmable timers that let you delay cooking up to two hours and then switch to "keep warm" for two hours post-cooking so you can leave the house for longer periods.

DOS	DON'TS
Always fill your slow cooker one-half to three-quarters full. If the appliance isn't sufficiently full the food may overcook and burn. If the appliance is overfilled, the food may undercook and may actually overflow.	Don't lift the lid to check on the food as it's cooking. This releases a lot of heat and increases the cooking time. Spin the lid while in place to remove condensation so you can see into the appliance.
Spray the ceramic insert with nonstick cooking spray or use a liner before you add food to it to make cleanup easier. The ceramic insert is smooth and is easy to clean, but food can stick, especially on the top edges.	Don't store leftovers in the insert. The thick walls prevent the food from cooling down quickly enough to prevent bacterial growth. Transfer leftover food to storage containers, such as zip-top bags or containers with snug lids.
The foods that take the longest to cook, usually root vegetables and beans, should be placed on the bottom of the insert where the heat is the strongest. More tender ingredients, such as peas and mushrooms, are placed on top.	Don't reheat leftovers in the slow cooker. The food has already been through the "danger zone" of 40°F to 140°F twice, and won't get hot enough quickly enough to kill any bacteria. Use the microwave, or reheat the food in a pan on the stove.
Cut similar foods into similar size pieces so they will cook at the same time. For instance, potatoes or parsnips should be sliced or cubed so they are the same size, while more tender vegetables such as bell peppers or asparagus should be the same size.	Don't add too much liquid to the slow cooker, especially at the beginning of cooking time. Foods give off liquid as they cook and the liquid will not evaporate in the slow cooker. Use the amount of liquid called for in the recipe.
If a sauce needs to be thickened, near the end of the cooking time, in a small bowl, mix to combine 1 tablespoon cornstarch or flour (for every cup of liquid in the slow cooker) with a few tablespoons room-temperature water or broth, and then stir that mixture into the food. Cover and cook on high for 10 to 15 minutes, or until the sauce reaches your desired thickness.	Don't stir the food in the slow cooker unless the recipe directs you to. Stirring can break down foods unnecessarily. And lifting the lid releases a lot of heat. Stir the food gently when cooking is finished, just before you're ready to eat.

THE BEST
of BEANS

BAKED BEANS

SERVES: 6 TO 8 • PREP TIME: 15 MINUTES, PLUS OVERNIGHT TO SOAK
COOK TIME: 8 TO 10 HOURS ON LOW

Baked Beans are a classic New England dish. This thrifty and wholesome recipe is perfect for the slow cooker. The beans simmer for hours, becoming tender and absorbing the wonderful rich flavors of the sauce. You do have to start this recipe the night before, since the beans must be soaked before they are cooked.

1. Sort the beans, rinse well, and drain. In a 4- or 5-quart slow cooker, cover the beans with cool water. Let stand overnight.

2. In the morning, drain the beans, discarding the soaking liquid. In the slow cooker, stir well to combine the beans, onion, garlic, Veggie Broth, tomato sauce, ketchup, molasses, brown sugar, mustard, vinegar, soy sauce, paprika, salt, and pepper.

3. Cover the slow cooker, and cook on low for 8 to 10 hours, or until the beans are tender.

4. Stir gently and serve.

The Next Day

Take it from me: These beans are even better the next day as the flavors meld together. Refrigerate the leftovers overnight. To reheat the next day, put the beans in a saucepan, stir in some Veggie Broth if necessary, and reheat just until the beans come to a boil.

1 pound dried navy beans

1 onion, chopped

3 garlic cloves, minced

2 cups Veggie Broth (page 60)

½ cup tomato sauce

½ cup ketchup

¼ cup molasses

⅓ cup brown sugar

3 tablespoons Dijon mustard

2 tablespoons apple cider vinegar

1 tablespoon soy sauce

1 teaspoon ground smoked paprika

1 teaspoon salt

½ teaspoon freshly ground black pepper

CHICKPEA SALAD *with* GREEN ONIONS *and* MINT

SERVES: 8 • PREP TIME: 20 MINUTES, PLUS OVERNIGHT TO SOAK • COOK TIME: 8 TO 11 HOURS ON LOW

Chickpeas, or garbanzo beans, are hearty but light in this simple salad. The dressing of green onions and mint is fresh and sweet and adds just the right amount of zing, and the sun-dried tomatoes bring all the flavors together with a burst of delight on your tongue.

1 (16-ounce) package dried chickpeas

6 cups Veggie Broth (page 60)

4 garlic cloves, minced

1 teaspoon salt

1 teaspoon dried mint leaves

⅛ teaspoon freshly ground black pepper

1 cup sliced green onions

1 cup sun-dried tomatoes in oil, chopped

3 tablespoons chopped fresh mint leaves

¾ cup extra-virgin olive oil

¼ cup freshly squeezed lemon juice

1. Sort the chickpeas, rinse well, and drain. In a 4- or 5-quart slow cooker, cover the chickpeas with cool water. Let stand overnight.

2. In the morning, drain the chickpeas, discarding the soaking liquid. In the slow cooker, combine the chickpeas, Veggie Broth, garlic, salt, mint, and pepper.

3. Cover and cook on low for 8 to 11 hours, or until the chickpeas are tender. Drain well.

4. In a large bowl, gently toss the hot chickpeas with the green onions, sun-dried tomatoes, and the fresh mint.

5. Drizzle with the olive oil and lemon juice, and toss to coat.

6. Serve immediately, or cover and chill for 2 to 4 hours before serving.

MAPLE BAKED BEANS

SERVES: 6 TO 8 • PREP TIME: 15 MINUTES, PLUS OVERNIGHT TO SOAK
COOK TIME: 8 TO 10 HOURS ON LOW

Maple syrup is the perfect partner for tender baked beans. The syrup is sweet but slightly smoky, too. Go for the real stuff, not maple-flavored pancake syrup. Look for "Grade B," which is less expensive, and as a bonus, the syrup is more flavorful.

1. Sort the beans, rinse well, and drain. In a 4- or 5-quart slow cooker, cover the beans with cool water. Let stand overnight.

2. In the morning, drain the beans, discarding the soaking liquid. In the slow cooker, stir well to combine the beans, onion, ginger, water, maple syrup, sugar, mustard, maple butter, salt, cloves, and pepper.

3. Cover and cook on low for 8 to 10 hours, or until the beans are tender.

4. Stir gently and serve.

- 1 pound dried navy beans
- 1 onion, chopped
- 2 tablespoons minced fresh ginger root
- 4½ cups water
- ⅔ cup maple syrup
- ¼ cup brown sugar or maple sugar
- 3 tablespoons Dijon mustard
- 2 tablespoons maple butter
- 1 teaspoon salt
- ¼ teaspoon ground cloves
- ¼ teaspoon freshly ground black pepper

Did You Know? Maple butter is made from maple syrup that has been boiled to concentrate it. It adds fabulous flavor to these beans. If you can't find it, substitute 1 tablespoon butter and increase the maple syrup to ¾ cup.

EDAMAME SUCCOTASH

SERVES: 6 TO 8 • PREP TIME: 15 MINUTES, PLUS OVERNIGHT TO SOAK
COOK TIME: 8 TO 10 HOURS ON LOW

Succotash was originated by the indigenous Narragansett people of what is now Rhode Island. Adopted by New England settlers, it is now commonly found on both sides of the Mason-Dixon line. It typically combines lima beans with corn, but I like using edamame, or soybeans, in place of the lima beans for an interesting twist that also adds more protein. Dried soybeans are tender and slightly sweet when slow cooked in this simple but delicious recipe.

1 pound dried soybeans

1 onion, chopped

3 celery stalks, sliced

2 garlic cloves, minced

1 tablespoon minced fresh ginger root

2 cups frozen corn

5 cups Veggie Broth (page 60)

2 large tomatoes, diced

1 dried bay leaf

1 teaspoon salt

⅛ teaspoon freshly ground black pepper

1. Sort the soybeans, rinse well, and drain. In a 4- or 5-quart slow cooker, cover the beans with cool water. Let stand overnight.

2. In the morning, drain the soybeans, discarding the soaking liquid. In the slow cooker, combine the soybeans, onion, celery, garlic, ginger, corn, Veggie Broth, tomatoes, bay leaf, salt, and pepper.

3. Cover and cook on low for 8 to 10 hours, or until the beans are tender.

4. Remove and discard the bay leaf, stir gently, and serve.

SPICY PINTO BEANS

SERVES: 6 TO 8 • PREP TIME: 15 MINUTES, PLUS OVERNIGHT TO SOAK
COOK TIME: 8 TO 10 HOURS ON LOW

These beans have a kick that makes them a great addition to tacos or salads, and the leftovers are the perfect start to making refried beans. Just mash the leftover beans and cook in extra-virgin olive oil in a saucepan over medium heat, stirring, until the mixture is thick.

1. Sort the beans, rinse well, and drain. In a 4- or 5-quart slow cooker, cover the beans with cool water. Let stand overnight.

2. In the morning, drain the beans, discarding the soaking liquid. In the slow cooker, stir well to combine the beans, onion, garlic, jalapeño, chili powder, cumin, salt, red pepper flakes, black pepper, bay leaf, and Veggie Broth.

3. Cover and cook on low for 8 to 10 hours, or until the beans are tender.

4. Remove and discard the bay leaf, stir gently, and serve.

1 pound dried pinto beans

1 onion, chopped

4 garlic cloves, minced

1 jalapeño pepper, minced

1 tablespoon chili powder

2 teaspoons ground cumin

1 teaspoon salt

½ teaspoon dried red pepper flakes

¼ teaspoon freshly ground black pepper

1 dried bay leaf

6 cups Veggie Broth (page 60) or water

THREE BEANS *and* BROWN RICE

SERVES: 6 TO 8 • PREP TIME: 15 MINUTES, PLUS OVERNIGHT TO SOAK
COOK TIME: 8 TO 10 HOURS ON LOW

Beans and rice is as classic a dish as they come. You can use any combination of beans in this slow cooker dish, but these three—kidney beans, black beans, and chickpeas—are a delicious combination.

1. Sort the kidney beans, black beans, and chickpeas, rinse well, and drain. In a 4- or 5-quart slow cooker, cover the beans and chickpeas with cool water. Let stand overnight.

2. In the morning, drain the beans and chickpeas, discarding the soaking liquid. In the slow cooker, combine the beans, chickpeas, rice, leek, garlic, carrots, Veggie Broth, water, marjoram, salt, and pepper.

3. Cover and cook on low for 8 to 10 hours, or until the beans, chickpeas, and rice are tender.

4. Gently stir in the Parmesan cheese and serve.

1 cup dried kidney beans

1 cup dried black beans

1 cup dried chickpeas (garbanzo beans)

1 cup long-grain brown rice

1 leek, chopped

2 garlic cloves, minced

3 carrots, sliced

5 cups Veggie Broth (page 60)

2 cups water

1 teaspoon dried marjoram leaves

1 teaspoon salt

⅛ teaspoon freshly ground black pepper

½ cup grated Parmesan cheese

BLACK BEANS *and* WILD RICE

SERVES: 6 TO 8 • PREP TIME: 15 MINUTES, PLUS OVERNIGHT TO SOAK
COOK TIME: 8 TO 10 HOURS ON LOW

Wild rice is not actually a rice but a whole grain. Wild rice plants grow in marshy areas in the upper Midwest. The rice takes a long time to cook, which makes it perfect for the slow cooker. Pairing wild rice with tender black beans in a smoky and rich sauce, this recipe is very satisfying.

1. Sort the beans, rinse well, and drain. In a 4- or 5-quart slow cooker, cover the beans with cool water. Let stand overnight.

2. In the morning, drain the beans, discarding the soaking liquid. In the slow cooker, stir well to combine the beans, wild rice, leek, red bell pepper, tomatoes, Veggie Broth, water, paprika, cumin, salt, and pepper.

3. Cover and cook on low for 8 to 10 hours, or until the beans and rice are tender.

4. Stir gently and serve.

1 pound dried black beans

1 cup wild rice

1 leek, chopped

1 red bell pepper, seeded and chopped

1 (14-ounce) can diced tomatoes, undrained

4 cups Veggie Broth (page 60)

3½ cups water

2 teaspoons ground smoked paprika

1 teaspoon ground cumin

1 teaspoon salt

¼ teaspoon freshly ground black pepper

Did You Know? Wild rice varies in quality. Look carefully at the package and choose only the package that has long, intact grains of rice. If the grains are broken, the rice will be mushy when it's cooked.

RICE *and* BLACK BEANS

SERVES: 6 TO 8 • PREP TIME: 15 MINUTES, PLUS OVERNIGHT TO SOAK
COOK TIME: 8 TO 10 HOURS ON LOW

Mild or spicy, this is a healthy and nutritious dish—full of fiber and complete protein. If you like things spicy, add more minced jalapeños, or use habanero peppers, which are a step up on the heat scale. For an additional depth of flavor, add chipotle chiles in adobo sauce.

1. Sort the beans, rinse well, and drain. In a 4- or 5-quart slow cooker, cover the beans with cool water. Let stand overnight.

2. In the morning, drain the beans, discarding the soaking liquid. In the slow cooker, stir well to combine the beans, rice, onion, garlic, jalapeño, Veggie Broth, water, salsa, chili powder, oregano, salt, black pepper, and red pepper flakes.

3. Cover and cook on low for 8 to 10 hours, or until the beans and rice are tender.

4. Stir gently and serve.

1 pound dried black beans

1 cup brown rice

1 onion, chopped

5 garlic cloves, sliced

2 jalapeño peppers, minced

5 cups Veggie Broth
  (page 60)

2 cups water

½ cup salsa

1 tablespoon chili powder

1 teaspoon dried
  oregano leaves

½ teaspoon salt

⅛ teaspoon freshly ground
  black pepper

⅛ teaspoon crushed red
  pepper flakes

Did You Know? Most of the heat in chile peppers is in the seeds and internal membranes. To reduce the heat level, remove and discard those parts. But if you like spicy foods, leave them in.

MEXICAN BLACK BEANS

SERVES: 6 TO 8 • PREP TIME: 20 MINUTES, PLUS OVERNIGHT TO SOAK
COOK TIME: 8 TO 10 HOURS ON LOW

The flavors of Mexico add great interest to a simple dish of black beans and some veggies. Chili powder, cumin, and chiles in adobo sauce can be found in most large grocery stores in the international foods aisle.

1. Sort the beans, rinse well, and drain. In a 4- or 5-quart slow cooker, cover the beans with cool water. Let stand overnight.

2. In the morning, drain the beans, discarding the soaking liquid. In the slow cooker, stir well to combine the beans, onion, tomatillos, garlic, jalapeño, chipotle chile, adobo sauce, tomatoes, Veggie Broth, water, chili powder, cumin, coriander, oregano, salt, and pepper.

3. Cover and cook on low for 8 to 10 hours, or until the beans are tender.

4. Stir gently and serve.

 Tomatillos are little green fruits that look very similar to tomatoes, and both are part of the nightshade family. Tomatillos have a tart and slightly spicy flavor that adds a wonderful taste to this simple recipe.

1 pound black beans

1 onion, chopped

3 tomatillos, husks removed, chopped

5 garlic cloves, minced

2 jalapeño or habanero peppers, minced

1 chipotle chile in adobo sauce, minced

2 tablespoons adobo sauce

2 cups chopped tomatoes

5 cups Veggie Broth (page 60)

1 cup water

1 tablespoon chili powder

1 teaspoon ground cumin

1 teaspoon ground coriander

1 teaspoon dried oregano leaves

1 teaspoon salt

⅛ teaspoon freshly ground black pepper

SMOKY BAKED BEANS

SERVES: 6 TO 8 • PREP TIME: 15 MINUTES, PLUS OVERNIGHT TO SOAK
COOK TIME: 8 TO 10 HOURS ON LOW

Smoke is a difficult flavor to achieve in vegetarian recipes, but I love to incorporate it when I can. Molasses, smoked paprika, and chipotle chiles in adobo sauce are easy additions that add that elusive taste. In a pinch, liquid smoke can be used, but it doesn't compare to the wonderful flavors of natural ingredients, especially when they are readily available.

1. Sort the Great Northern and navy beans, rinse well, and drain. In a 4- or 5-quart slow cooker, cover the beans with cool water. Let stand overnight.

2. In the morning, drain the beans, discarding the soaking liquid. In the slow cooker, stir well to combine the beans, Veggie Broth, onions, garlic, chipotle chiles, adobo sauce, tomato sauce, brown sugar, ketchup, vinegar, mustard, molasses, paprika, salt, and pepper.

3. Cover and cook on low for 8 to 10 hours, or until the beans and rice are tender.

4. Stir gently and serve.

 Chipotle chiles in adobo are smoked jalapeños packed in a spicy red sauce. Both the chiles and the sauce are great additions to many bean slow cooker recipes. They add wonderful, unexpected depth of flavor.

½ pound dried Great Northern beans

½ pound dried navy beans

5 cups Veggie Broth (page 60)

2 onions, chopped

3 garlic cloves, minced

2 chipotle chiles in adobo sauce, minced

2 tablespoons adobo sauce

1 (8-ounce) can tomato sauce

½ cup brown sugar

½ cup ketchup

¼ cup red wine vinegar

¼ cup Dijon mustard

¼ cup molasses

2 teaspoons ground smoked paprika

1 teaspoon salt

¼ teaspoon freshly ground black pepper

HOPPIN' JOHN

SERVES: 6 TO 8 • PREP TIME: 15 MINUTES, PLUS OVERNIGHT TO SOAK
COOK TIME: 8 TO 10 HOURS ON LOW

Hoppin' John is a classic Southern dish of black-eyed peas with rice traditionally eaten on New Year's Day for good luck. The recipe usually includes bacon or smoked sausage, but here we get that wonderful rich flavor with hearty vegetables such as mushrooms and onions, along with tomato paste and a bay leaf. A bit of vegetarian sausage makes the flavor that much more complex.

1. Sort the peas, rinse well, and drain. In a 4- or 5-quart slow cooker, cover the peas with cool water. Let stand overnight.

2. In the morning, drain the peas, discarding the soaking liquid. In the slow cooker, stir well to combine the peas, rice, onion, mushrooms, garlic, Veggie Broth, meatless Italian sausage, diced tomatoes, tomato paste, bay leaf, salt, and pepper.

3. Cover and cook on low for 8 to 10 hours, or until the beans and rice are tender.

4. Remove and discard the bay leaf, stir gently, and serve.

1 pound dried black-eyed peas

1½ cups brown rice

1 onion, chopped

1 cup chopped cremini mushrooms

4 garlic cloves, sliced

6 cups Veggie Broth (page 60)

2 meatless Italian sausages, chopped

1 (14-ounce) can diced tomatoes, undrained

3 tablespoons tomato paste

1 dried bay leaf

1 teaspoon salt

¼ teaspoon freshly ground pepper

Ingredient Tip Cremini mushrooms are baby portobello mushrooms. A rich brown color, these small mushrooms provide more flavor than white button mushrooms. You can find them in most grocery stores.

TOFU BEAN BAKE

SERVES: 6 TO 8 • PREP TIME: 15 MINUTES, PLUS OVERNIGHT TO SOAK
COOK TIME: 8 TO 10 HOURS ON LOW

Tofu and beans combine to make the perfect protein source. I like to use firm tofu in slow cooker beans, soups, stews, and chili because it keeps its shape during the long cooking time. The key is to always drain tofu well and press it between paper towels to remove excess moisture.

1. Sort the beans, rinse well, and drain. In a 4- or 5-quart slow cooker, cover the beans with cool water. Let stand overnight.

2. In the morning, drain the beans, discarding the soaking liquid.

3. In a colander, drain the tofu for 5 minutes. Then put the tofu block between paper towels and press gently to remove excess water. Cut the tofu into ½-inch cubes.

4. In the slow cooker, stir well to combine the beans, tofu cubes, leek, Veggie Broth, tomatoes with green chiles, tomato paste, chipotle chile, adobo sauce, curry powder, salt, and pepper.

5. Cover and cook on low for 8 to 10 hours, or until the beans are tender.

6. Stir gently and serve.

- 1 cup dried kidney beans
- 1 cup dried navy beans
- 1 (12-ounce) package firm tofu
- 1 leek, chopped
- 4 cups Veggie Broth (page 60)
- 1 (14-ounce) can diced tomatoes with green chiles, undrained
- 3 tablespoons tomato paste
- 1 chipotle chile in adobo sauce, minced
- 1 tablespoon adobo sauce
- 1 teaspoon curry powder
- ½ teaspoon salt
- ⅛ teaspoon freshly ground black pepper

Seasonal Substitute If you grow tomatoes in your backyard, or buy them from a farmers' market in the summer, substitute two large ripe red tomatoes for the canned tomatoes. Add a minced fresh jalapeño or two as well for a subtle kick of heat.

SWEET *and* SPICY BEANS

SERVES: 6 TO 8 • PREP TIME: 15 MINUTES, PLUS OVERNIGHT TO SOAK
COOK TIME: 8 TO 10 HOURS ON LOW

Sriracha is a hot sauce made from chile peppers, vinegar, sugar, salt, and lots of garlic. If you like spicy foods, it definitely deserves a place in your pantry. Here it is balanced with honey, herbs, and spices to transform plain old beans into a special dish.

1. Sort the beans, rinse well, and drain. In a 4- or 5-quart slow cooker, cover the beans with cool water. Let stand overnight.

2. In the morning, drain the beans, discarding the soaking liquid. In the slow cooker, stir well to combine the beans, Veggie Broth, apple juice, onion, poblano, garlic, ginger, Sriracha, honey, brown sugar, tomato sauce, marjoram, salt, and red pepper flakes.

3. Cover and cook on low for 8 to 10 hours, or until the beans are tender.

4. Stir gently and serve.

1 cup dried pinto beans

1 cup dried kidney beans

1 cup dried black beans

5 cups Veggie Broth (page 60)

1 cup apple juice

1 onion, finely chopped

1 poblano pepper, chopped

3 garlic cloves, minced

2 tablespoons minced fresh ginger root

2 tablespoons Sriracha sauce

½ cup honey

⅓ cup brown sugar

1 (8-ounce) can tomato sauce

1 teaspoon dried marjoram leaves

½ teaspoon salt

⅛ teaspoon crushed red pepper flakes

MOROCCAN THREE-BEAN MEDLEY

SERVES: 6 TO 8 • PREP TIME: 15 MINUTES, PLUS OVERNIGHT TO SOAK
COOK TIME: 8 TO 10 HOURS ON LOW

In Morocco, white beans are often stewed with tomatoes and spices and served as a vegetarian entrée. You can use any combination of dried navy beans, cannellini beans, lima beans, garbanzo beans, white kidney beans, or Great Northern beans for a delicious taste of North Africa.

1. Sort the beans, rinse well, and drain. In a 4- or 5-quart slow cooker, cover the beans with cool water. Let stand overnight.

2. In the morning, drain the beans, discarding the soaking liquid. In the slow cooker, stir well to combine the beans, olive oil, onion, leek, garlic, tomato, tomato sauce, Veggie Broth, coriander, cumin, paprika, turmeric, curry powder, bay leaf, salt, and pepper.

3. Cover and cook on low for 8 to 10 hours, or until the beans are tender.

4. Remove and discard the bay leaf, stir gently, and serve.

1 cup dried white kidney beans

1 cup dried navy beans

1 cup dried Great Northern beans

¼ cup extra-virgin olive oil

1 onion, chopped

1 leek, chopped

4 garlic cloves, minced

1 tomato, chopped

1 (8-ounce) can tomato sauce

6 cups Veggie Broth (page 60)

1 teaspoon dried coriander

1 teaspoon ground cumin

1 teaspoon ground smoked paprika

1 teaspoon ground turmeric

1 teaspoon curry powder

1 dried bay leaf

½ teaspoon salt

⅛ teaspoon freshly ground black pepper

SPICY BLACK-EYED PEAS

SERVES: 6 TO 8 • PREP TIME: 10 MINUTES, PLUS OVERNIGHT TO SOAK
COOK TIME: 8 TO 10 HOURS ON LOW

Cajun seasoning can be found in most grocery stores. It's usually a blend of salt, onion and garlic powders, paprika, several kinds of dried peppers, oregano, and thyme. This seasoning blend is quite spicy; try a few to find your favorite, or create your own.

1. Sort the peas, rinse well, and drain. In a 4- or 5-quart slow cooker, cover the beans with cool water. Let stand overnight.

2. In the morning, drain the beans, discarding the soaking liquid. In the slow cooker, stir well to combine the beans, Veggie Broth, onions, garlic, Cajun seasoning, tomatoes, jalapeño, chipotle chile, adobo sauce, salt, black pepper, and red pepper flakes.

3. Cover and cook on low for 8 to 10 hours, or until the beans are tender.

4. Taste for seasoning, stir gently, and serve.

1 pound dried black-eyed peas

5 cups Veggie Broth (page 60)

2 onions, chopped

4 garlic cloves, minced

1½ teaspoons Cajun seasoning

2 large tomatoes, chopped

1 jalapeño pepper, minced

1 chipotle chile in adobo sauce, minced

2 tablespoons adobo sauce

½ teaspoon salt

⅛ teaspoon freshly ground black pepper

⅛ teaspoon crushed red pepper flakes

Did You Know? You may be wondering what a recipe with no beans is doing in the beans chapter. Although they are called peas, these legumes are actually beans.

THE GREATEST
of GRAINS

AMARANTH PILAF

SERVES: 6 TO 8 • PREP TIME: 15 MINUTES • COOK TIME: 6 TO 8 HOURS ON LOW

Although it is called a grain, amaranth is actually a seed, which makes it great for those who cannot eat gluten. It is known as an "ancient seed" because it has been used for more than 8,000 years. Flavored with leeks, celery, onions, and garlic, this pilaf is perfect for a light supper.

1. In a 4- or 5-quart slow cooker, gently combine the amaranth, onion, leek, celery, garlic, Veggie Broth, salt, pepper, thyme, and basil.

2. Cover and cook on low for 6 to 8 hours, or until the amaranth is tender.

3. Stir gently and serve.

2 cups amaranth

1 onion, chopped

1 leek, chopped

3 celery stalks, sliced

3 garlic cloves, sliced

6 cups Veggie Broth (page 60)

1 teaspoon salt

¼ teaspoon freshly ground black pepper

1 teaspoon dried thyme leaves

1 teaspoon dried basil leaves

VEGGIE-QUINOA BAKE

SERVES 6 TO 8 • PREP TIME: 20 MINUTES • COOK TIME: 7 TO 8 HOURS ON LOW

Quinoa (pronounced "keen-wah") is another ancient grain that is very good for you and is high in protein. It does have a bitter-tasting coating called saponin, so it's always best to rinse quinoa before you cook it. White, red, and black quinoa is available in most supermarkets.

2 cups quinoa

1 onion, chopped

3 carrots, sliced

2 tomatoes, chopped

3 celery stalks, sliced

4 garlic cloves, minced

4 cups Veggie Broth (page 60)

1 teaspoon salt

⅛ teaspoon freshly ground black pepper

1 teaspoon dried oregano leaves

1 teaspoon dried basil leaves

1. In a fine strainer, run cool water over the quinoa grains for a few minutes. Drain well.

2. In a 4-quart slow cooker, stir well to combine the quinoa, onion, carrots, tomatoes, celery, garlic, Veggie Broth, salt, pepper, oregano, and basil.

3. Cover and cook on low for 7 to 8 hours, or until the quinoa is tender.

4. Stir gently and serve.

While quinoa does not have gluten, it does have some proteins that are similar to the proteins found in wheat and barley. If you have celiac disease or a gluten intolerance, it's best to avoid this grain.

WHEAT BERRIES *with* SQUASH

SERVES: 6 TO 8 • PREP TIME: 20 MINUTES • COOK TIME: 6 TO 8 HOURS ON LOW

Wheat berries are actually whole, unprocessed kernels of wheat. They are not commonly eaten in the United States, but they should be! When cooked, the berries are tender and chewy with the most wonderful flavor. They are full of fiber and lots of vitamins—especially B vitamins—and minerals.

1. In a 4- or 5-quart slow cooker, stir well to combine the wheat berries, shallots, squash, Veggie Broth, apple juice, salt, pepper, and ginger.

2. Cover and cook on low for 6 to 8 hours, or until the wheat berries and squash are tender.

3. Gently stir in the butter and Parmesan cheese, and serve.

Ingredient Tip There are several types of squash you can use in this recipe. Butternut squash is the sweetest, but also try pumpkin, acorn squash, buttercup, or Blue Hubbard.

2 cups wheat berries

3 shallots, chopped

3 cups cubed butternut squash

6 cups Veggie Broth (page 60)

1 cup apple juice

1 teaspoon salt

¼ teaspoon freshly ground black pepper

½ teaspoon ground ginger

2 tablespoons butter

⅓ cup grated Parmesan cheese

THREE-GRAIN MEDLEY

SERVES: 6 TO 8 • PREP TIME: 15 MINUTES • COOK TIME: 6 TO 8 HOURS ON LOW

Combining grains in a flavorful broth with vegetables makes a satisfying main dish. Chewy hulled barley, amaranth, and wheat berries are delicious, and they create a hearty dish full of wonderful textures.

1. In a 4- or 5-quart slow cooker, stir well to combine the wheat berries, barley, amaranth, onion, mushrooms, red bell peppers, garlic, Veggie Broth, marjoram, oregano, salt, and pepper.

2. Cover and cook on low for 6 to 8 hours, or until the grains are tender.

3. Gently stir in the olive oil, and serve.

1 cup wheat berries

1 cup hulled barley

1 cup amaranth

1 onion, chopped

2 cups sliced mushrooms

2 red bell peppers, seeded and chopped

3 garlic cloves, minced

5½ cups Veggie Broth (page 60)

1 teaspoon dried marjoram leaves

1 teaspoon dried oregano leaves

1 teaspoon salt

¼ teaspoon freshly ground black pepper

2 tablespoons olive oil

BARLEY-ONION PILAF

SERVES: 6 TO 8 • PREP TIME: 15 MINUTES • COOK TIME: 7 TO 8 HOURS ON LOW

A pilaf is a mixture of grains—usually rice—cooked with vegetables until tender. I like to serve this version made with barley for lunch or a simple dinner. Hulled barley cooks very well in the slow cooker, and it's a great source of fiber, B vitamins, and minerals like manganese.

1. In a 4- or 5-quart slow cooker, stir well to combine the barley, yellow onion, red onion, garlic, Veggie Broth, lemon juice, salt, marjoram, rosemary sprig, and pepper.

2. Cover and cook on low for 7 to 8 hours, or until the barley is tender.

3. Remove the rosemary stem (the leaves should have fallen off into the pilaf), stir gently, and serve.

2 cups hulled barley

1 yellow onion, chopped

1 red onion, chopped

5 garlic cloves, minced

8 cups Veggie Broth (page 60) or water

2 tablespoons freshly squeezed lemon juice

1 teaspoon salt

1 teaspoon dried marjoram leaves

1 fresh rosemary sprig

⅛ teaspoon freshly ground black pepper

Ingredient Tip Hulled barley is best for the slow cooker, since it only has the outer husk removed. Pearl barley can be used, but the cooking time should be cut in half.

HEIRLOOM BLACK *and* RED RICE *with* PUMPKIN SEEDS *and* SAGE

SERVES 6 TO 8 • PREP TIME: 15 MINUTES • COOK TIME: 6 HOURS ON LOW

Black rice and red rice are full of healthy antioxidants, and they are gorgeous and have the best flavor. You can substitute other veggies in this recipe if you'd like. Think about adding freshly picked chopped zucchini, yellow summer squash, or green beans.

1½ cups black rice

1½ cups red rice

1 onion, chopped

4 garlic cloves, minced

6 cups Veggie Broth (page 60)

1 teaspoon dried sage leaves

1 teaspoon salt

⅛ teaspoon freshly ground black pepper

2 cups toasted pumpkin seeds

2 tablespoons chopped fresh sage leaves

1. In a 4-quart slow cooker, combine the black rice, red rice, onion, garlic, Veggie Broth, sage, salt, and pepper.

2. Cover and cook on low for 6 hours, or until the rice is tender.

3. Gently stir in the pumpkin seeds and fresh sage, and serve.

QUINOA TABBOULEH SALAD

SERVES: 6 TO 8 • PREP TIME: 20 MINUTES • COOK TIME: 3 TO 4 HOURS ON LOW

Quinoa makes for a wonderful and healthy salad, with lots of fiber. When paired with fresh vegetables, it becomes a great light lunch, or a perfect side for dinner. The lemony mustard dressing adds the perfect finishing touch.

1. In a 4- or 5-quart slow cooker, stir well to combine the bulgur, leek, onion, garlic, yellow and red bell peppers, zucchini, Veggie Broth, thyme, basil, salt, and pepper.

2. Cover and cook on low for 3 to 4 hours, or until the bulgur and vegetables are tender.

3. Drain if necessary, and transfer the bulgur and vegetables to a large bowl.

4. In a small bowl, mix well to combine the olive oil, lemon juice, and mustard. Pour the dressing over the bulgur and vegetables, and stir gently to mix.

5. Serve immediately, or cover and chill for 2 to 4 hours before serving.

2 cups bulgur

1 leek, chopped

1 onion, chopped

3 garlic cloves, minced

2 yellow bell peppers, seeded and sliced

2 red bell peppers, seeded and chopped

2 zucchini, sliced

4 cups Veggie Broth (page 60)

1 teaspoon dried thyme leaves

1 teaspoon dried basil leaves

1 teaspoon salt

⅛ teaspoon freshly ground black pepper

⅔ cup extra-virgin olive oil

3 tablespoons freshly squeezed lemon juice

3 tablespoons Dijon mustard

BROWN RICE RISOTTO

SERVES 6 TO 8 • PREP TIME: 15 MINUTES • COOK TIME: 5 TO 6 HOURS ON LOW

Risotto is a creamy Italian dish made from rice that is slowly cooked while you stir constantly. Use a slow cooker instead, and you won't have to stir much at all! Arborio rice is the key to a successful risotto, and you can find brown Arborio rice in most large grocery stores or order it online.

2 cups brown Arborio rice

1 onion, finely chopped

1 leek, finely chopped

3 garlic cloves, minced

4 cups Veggie Broth (page 60)

1 cup water

1 teaspoon salt

1 teaspoon dried marjoram leaves

½ teaspoon dried oregano leaves

2 tablespoons butter

½ cup grated Parmesan cheese

1. In a 4-quart slow cooker, stir well to combine the rice, onion, leek, garlic, Veggie Broth, water, salt, marjoram, and oregano.

2. Cover and cook on low for 5 to 6 hours, or until the rice is tender and the mixture is creamy. Stir once during cooking time if you are home; if not, don't worry about it.

3. Stir in the butter and cheese, and cook on low for another 5 to 10 minutes.

4. Stir gently and serve.

Did You Know? Short-grain Arborio rice has a specific type of starch called amylopectin that makes risotto creamy. The starch is released as the rice cooks. Long-grain and medium-grain rice will not work as well.

RED RICE PILAF

SERVES 6 TO 8 • PREP TIME: 15 MINUTES • COOK TIME: 4½ TO 5½ HOURS ON LOW

There are so many different colors of rice on the market. Go to a big grocery store, and spend some time browsing through the aisle to see what you can find. Red rice is high in anthocyanin, a phytochemical that may help prevent cancer. The color is really red!

1. In a 4-quart slow cooker, stir well to combine the rice, olive oil, mushrooms, shallots, garlic, Veggie Broth, thyme, bay leaf, salt, and pepper.

2. Cover and cook on low for 4½ to 5½ hours, or until the rice is tender.

3. Stir gently and serve.

2 cups red rice

1 tablespoon olive oil

2 cups sliced cremini mushrooms

2 shallots, minced

3 garlic cloves, minced

3½ cups Veggie Broth (page 60)

1 teaspoon dried thyme leaves

1 dried bay leaf

1 teaspoon salt

⅛ teaspoon freshly ground black pepper

KASHA VARNISHKES

SERVES: 6 TO 8 • PREP TIME: 15 MINUTES
COOK TIME: 6 TO 8 HOURS ON LOW, PLUS 30 TO 40 MINUTES ON HIGH

Buckwheat groats, also known as kasha, are triangular seeds of the buckwheat plant, a member of the rhubarb family. Because it's a seed, it does not contain any gluten (admittedly confusing, given its name). In this classic Eastern European staple, the pasta is stirred in at the very end, to keep it from overcooking.

1. In a 4-quart slow cooker, combine the onions, mushrooms, garlic, olive oil, salt, pepper, Veggie Broth, and groats.

2. Cover and cook on low for 6 to 8 hours, or until groats are tender.

3. Add the pasta, and stir well. Cover and cook on high for about 30 to 40 minutes, or until the pasta is tender.

4. Stir gently and serve.

4 onions, chopped

2 cups sliced cremini mushrooms

3 garlic cloves, sliced

2 tablespoons olive oil

1 teaspoon salt

¼ teaspoon freshly ground black pepper

5 cups Veggie Broth (page 60)

2 cups buckwheat groats, rinsed and drained

2 cups bowtie pasta

Did You Know? Kasha Varnishkes is a dish that is part of the Ashkenazi Jewish culture. The traditional recipe is prepared with poultry fat, though we've substituted olive oil here.

BLACK RICE *and* SQUASH BAKE

SERVES 6 TO 8 • PREP TIME: 15 MINUTES • COOK TIME: 5 TO 6 HOURS ON LOW

Black rice, also known as Forbidden Rice, used to be reserved for royalty in China. Now everyone can enjoy this unusual and delicious grain, as it's available in many large grocery stores or online. The contrast of the black rice and yellow-orange squash in this dish makes for a striking presentation.

1. In a 4-quart slow cooker, stir well to combine the rice, leek, garlic, ginger, squash, Veggie Broth, olive oil, salt, pepper, and cumin.

2. Cover and cook on low for 5 to 6 hours, or until the rice and vegetables are tender.

3. Stir gently and serve.

2 cups black rice

1 leek, chopped

3 garlic cloves, minced

1 tablespoon grated fresh ginger root

3 cups cubed butternut squash

5 cups Veggie Broth (page 60)

2 tablespoons olive oil

1 teaspoon salt

⅛ teaspoon freshly ground black pepper

1 teaspoon ground cumin

CARBONARA RISOTTO

SERVES: 6 TO 8 • PREP TIME: 15 MINUTES
COOK TIME: 5 HOURS, 10 MINUTES TO 6 HOURS, 15 MINUTES ON LOW

Carbonara is one of my favorite dishes. The combination of egg, cream, and cheese adds richness to plain old pasta. Risotto gets the same treatment in this easy recipe, transforming it into a lush and delicious special recipe.

1. In a 4-quart slow cooker, stir well to combine the rice, mushrooms, onion, garlic, Veggie Broth, salt, pepper, and thyme.

2. Cover and cook on low for 5 to 6 hours, or until the rice is tender.

3. Stir in the peas.

4. In a small bowl, beat the eggs and cream together. Stir the mixture into the slow cooker, and then stir in the Parmesan cheese.

5. Cover and cook on low for another 10 to 15 minutes, or until hot.

6. Sit gently and serve.

- 3 cups short-grain brown rice
- 2 cups sliced cremini mushrooms
- 1 onion, chopped
- 2 garlic cloves, minced
- 5 cups Veggie Broth (page 60)
- 1 teaspoon salt
- ⅛ teaspoon freshly ground black pepper
- 1 teaspoon dried thyme leaves
- 2 cups frozen baby peas, thawed
- 2 eggs, beaten
- ⅓ cup light cream
- ½ cup grated Parmesan cheese

 The Next Day Leftover risotto makes wonderful little risotto cakes. Just form the cold mixture into patties, dip into a beaten egg, and cover with bread crumbs. Melt a little butter in a frying pan over medium-high heat, add the risotto patties, and fry until golden brown on both sides.

BARLEY-VEGETABLE RISOTTO

SERVES: 6 TO 8 • PREP TIME: 15 MINUTES
COOK TIME: 6 TO 8 HOURS ON LOW, PLUS 20 MINUTES ON THE STOVE TOP

Barley risotto is delicious, although it doesn't achieve the creaminess of a true rice-based risotto. That's okay—I add some light cream to give the sauce a velvety texture.

1. In a large skillet over medium heat, heat the olive oil. Sauté the onion until it starts to brown, 10 to 15 minutes.

2. Add the barley, and cook, stirring, until it is toasted, 2 to 4 minutes.

3. Add 1 cup of Veggie Broth, and bring it to a simmer. Turn off the heat.

4. Transfer the mixture to a 4- to 6-quart slow cooker. Add the mushrooms, garlic, salt, pepper, and the remaining 3 cups of Veggie Broth, and stir well.

5. Cover and cook on low for 6 to 8 hours, or until the barley is tender.

6. Stir in the cheese, butter, and cream. Cover, turn off the slow cooker, and let the risotto stand for 10 minutes.

7. Stir gently and serve.

1 tablespoon olive oil

1 onion, finely chopped

2 cups hulled barley

4 cups Veggie Broth (page 60), divided

2 cups sliced button mushrooms

3 cloves garlic, minced

1 teaspoon salt

1/8 teaspoon freshly ground black pepper

1 cup grated Parmesan cheese

2 tablespoons butter

1/3 cup light cream

CHIPOTLE GRITS

SERVES: 6 TO 8 • PREP TIME: 20 MINUTES • COOK TIME: 7 TO 8 HOURS ON LOW

Little else says Southern like grits. They are usually cooked with lots of butter and cream. This recipe is spicier than most grits recipes—the chipotle chiles give it a heat kick—and it has lots of veggies for more nutrition, color, and flavor.

1. In a 4- or 5-quart slow cooker, stir well to combine the grits, onion, mushrooms, red and yellow bell peppers, chipotle chiles, adobo sauce, garlic, Veggie Broth, salt, and pepper.

2. Cover and cook on low for 7 to 8 hours, or until the grits are tender.

3. Stir in the cream and incorporate the Havarti and Parmesan cheeses. Turn off the slow cooker, cover, and let the grits stand for 10 minutes.

4. Stir gently and serve.

Never use instant grits in the slow cooker—it's a recipe for unappetizing mushiness. In fact, Southern cooks say never use instant grits at all. Stone-ground grits have a better texture, a rich flavor, and take longer to cook.

2 cups stone-ground yellow or white grits

1 onion, chopped

2 cups sliced mushrooms

1 red bell pepper, seeded and chopped

1 yellow bell pepper, seeded and chopped

2 chipotle chiles in adobo sauce, minced

2 tablespoons adobo sauce

4 garlic cloves, minced

6 cups Veggie Broth (page 60) or water

1 teaspoon salt

1/8 teaspoon freshly ground black pepper

1 cup light cream

1 1/2 cups shredded Havarti or Swiss cheese

1/4 cup grated Parmesan cheese

SPANISH WILD RICE

SERVES: 6 TO 8 • PREP TIME: 15 MINUTES • COOK TIME: 6 TO 8 HOURS ON LOW

Spanish rice is white rice cooked with tomatoes to give it its characteristic red color, but I like to shake things up and make it with wild rice. This seed stands up well to this long, slow method of cooking. Adding lots of veggies makes it a hearty, healthier dish.

1. In a 4- or 5-quart slow cooker, stir well to combine the rice, onion, bell pepper, garlic, chipotle chiles, adobo sauce, Veggie Broth, diced tomatoes, tomato paste, chili powder, oregano, salt, cayenne pepper, and black pepper.

2. Cover and cook on low for 6 to 8 hours, or until the wild rice is tender.

3. Stir gently and serve.

2 cups wild rice, rinsed and drained

1 onion, chopped

2 green bell peppers, seeded and chopped

4 garlic cloves, sliced

2 chipotle chiles in adobo sauce, minced

2 tablespoons adobo sauce

4 cups Veggie Broth (page 60)

1 (14-ounce) can diced tomatoes, undrained

3 tablespoons tomato paste

1 tablespoon chili powder

1 teaspoon dried oregano leaves

½ teaspoon salt

⅛ teaspoon ground cayenne pepper

⅛ teaspoon freshly ground black pepper

BROTHS & SAUCES

VEGGIE BROTH

MAKES 12 CUPS • PREP TIME: 15 MINUTES • COOK TIME: 8 TO 10 HOURS ON LOW

This broth is used in many recipes in this book. A good broth should be deeply flavored and rich, and a good vegetable broth uses ingredients such as celery, onions, and mushrooms to build that great depth of flavor. While you can buy some fairly good boxed broths, the canned ones are usually tinny-tasting and too salty. This broth freezes well (up to 4 months), making it great to have in reserve to use in slow cooker recipes.

4 carrots, chopped

5 celery stalks, chopped

3 onions, unpeeled, sliced

4 large tomatoes, chopped

2 cups sliced cremini mushrooms

6 garlic cloves, sliced

1 teaspoon salt

1 teaspoon black peppercorns

½ teaspoon green peppercorns

1 fresh thyme sprig

1 dried bay leaf

10 cups water

1. In a 5-quart slow cooker, stir well to combine the carrots, celery, onions, tomatoes, mushrooms, garlic, salt, black and green peppercorns, thyme, bay leaf, and water.

2. Cover and cook on low for 8 to 10 hours, or until the broth tastes rich and well-seasoned. Add more salt or thyme if you'd like.

3. Strain the broth into a large container, discarding the solids. Let the broth cool for 20 minutes, and refrigerate in an airtight container.

4. To freeze, portion the cooled broth into 1-cup containers, label with the name of the recipe and the date it was made, and freeze up to 4 months. To use, thaw in the refrigerator overnight or put the broth straight into a slow cooker to use in a recipe.

Perfect Pair

This broth makes a really easy miso soup with the addition of a handful of sliced button mushrooms, 1 tablespoon of miso, and a garnish of chopped chives. It's a delicious vegan and nut-free lunch or first course.

ROASTED ROOT VEGETABLE BROTH

MAKES 12 CUPS • PREP TIME: 20 MINUTES • COOK TIME: 10 TO 14 HOURS ON LOW

This recipe takes a bit longer than most because the vegetables are first roasted in the slow cooker, then all the flavor goodness is extracted with some water and additional cooking time. None of the vegetables need to be peeled in this recipe; just scrub them under cool running water, and into the slow cooker they go.

1. In a 6-quart slow cooker, stir to combine the carrots, celery, mushrooms, onion, parsnip, and olive oil.

2. Cover and cook on low for 6 to 8 hours, or until the vegetables are roasted.

3. Add the water, tomatoes, thyme, salt, and peppercorns, and stir.

4. Cover and cook on low for 4 to 6 hours longer, or until the broth tastes rich.

5. Add more salt or thyme if you'd like. Strain the broth into a large container, discarding the solids.

6. Let the broth cool for 30 minutes, and then cover tightly and refrigerate. Use within 1 week, or freeze for longer storage.

4 carrots, unpeeled, cut into chunks

4 celery stalks, unpeeled, halved

3 large portobello mushrooms, halved

2 onions, unpeeled, sliced

1 parsnip, unpeeled, cut into thick slices

2 tablespoons olive oil

11 cups water

2 tomatoes, chopped

2 fresh thyme sprigs

1 teaspoon salt

½ teaspoon black peppercorns

Did You Know? Any recipe called a "broth" is made without meat or poultry bones. Recipes called "stock" are made with bones. So no vegetarian broth should ever be called a stock, though this designation has been slightly muddled by the bone broth trend.

APPLE BUTTER

MAKES 6 CUPS • PREP TIME: 25 MINUTES
COOK TIME: 6 HOURS ON HIGH, PLUS 12 TO 14 HOURS ON LOW

Thick, fragrant, and irresistible, apple butter is a concentrated form of applesauce. It's wonderful served on toasted whole-grain bread in the morning, and you can add it to apple pies for a fabulous flavor boost. It cooks for a very long time in the slow cooker, resulting in a beautiful brown color and rich flavor.

15 cups peeled, cored, and chopped tart apples, such as Granny Smith or McIntosh

½ cup freshly squeezed lemon juice

½ teaspoon salt

⅔ cup honey

⅔ cup firmly packed brown sugar

½ cup granulated sugar

1 tablespoon ground cinnamon

½ teaspoon ground cloves

½ teaspoon ground nutmeg

⅛ teaspoon ground cardamom

2 teaspoons vanilla

1. In a 6- or 7-quart slow cooker, stir to combine the apples, lemon juice, and salt. Cover and cook on high for 6 hours.

2. Stir the apples, turn the slow cooker to low, and cook for another 8 to 9 hours, or until the apples are very soft and light brown.

3. Stir in the honey, brown sugar, granulated sugar, cinnamon, cloves, nutmeg, and cardamom.

4. Cover and cook on low for another 4 to 5 hours, or until the apple butter is deep brown.

5. Stir the apple butter and taste it. If it tastes rich, it's done. If it still tastes a little weak or if it's thinner than you'd like, remove the cover and cook, uncovered, on low for another 1 to 2 hours. Once it reaches your desired taste and consistency, stir in the vanilla.

6. Let the apple butter cool in a large container for 1 hour at room temperature, and then cover and refrigerate for up to a week. Freeze in 1-cup portions for longer storage.

 In season, pears are also wonderful in this recipe. Cut down on the sugar a bit, though, since pears are usually sweeter than apples. You may want to reduce the cinnamon, too.

SWEET PEAR SAUCE

MAKES 6 CUPS • PREP TIME: 25 MINUTES • COOK TIME: 7 TO 8 HOURS ON LOW

Pear sauce is a nice alternative to the ubiquitous applesauce. The flavor is more interesting than typical fruit sauces as its flavors are more complex. This sauce freezes well, too. Oh, and if you love applesauce, go ahead and make it according to this recipe!

12 pears, peeled, cored, and chopped

½ cup water

3 tablespoons freshly squeezed lemon juice

3 tablespoons honey

3 tablespoons maple syrup

1 teaspoon ground cinnamon, plus more if desired

⅛ teaspoon salt

2 teaspoons vanilla

1. In a 4-quart slow cooker, stir to combine the pears, water, lemon juice, honey, maple syrup, cinnamon, and salt.

2. Cover and cook on low for 7 to 8 hours, or until the pears are very soft.

3. Uncover and mash the pears using a potato masher or immersion blender right in the slow cooker.

4. Stir in the vanilla, taste for seasoning, and add more cinnamon if you'd like.

5. Let the sauce cool to room temperature, and then cover and refrigerate for up to a week. Freeze for longer storage.

MARINARA SAUCE

MAKES 8 CUPS • PREP TIME: 15 MINUTES • COOK TIME: 7 TO 8 HOURS ON LOW

Marinara is a basic Italian tomato sauce typically served over pasta. It's made with onions, garlic, and herbs and can include olives. This simple recipe should be in your repertoire and in your freezer. Once you have the homemade kind, you'll never want a jarred product again.

1. In a 4- or 5-quart slow cooker, stir well to combine the crushed tomatoes, diced tomatoes, tomato paste, onion, garlic, olive oil, honey, Veggie Broth, wine (if using), bay leaf, oregano, basil, salt, and pepper.

2. Cover and cook on low for 7 to 8 hours, or until the sauce tastes rich.

3. Remove and discard the bay leaf. You can purée the sauce right in the slow cooker using an immersion blender, or, if you like it slightly chunkier, crush some of the tomatoes with a potato masher.

4. Cool and refrigerate for up to 1 week, or freeze for longer storage.

- 1 (28-ounce) can crushed tomatoes
- 2 (14-ounce) cans diced tomatoes, undrained
- 1 (6-ounce) can tomato paste
- 2 onions, finely chopped
- 5 garlic cloves, minced
- 2 tablespoons olive oil
- 2 tablespoons honey
- 1 cup Veggie Broth (page 60)
- ½ cup dry red wine (optional) or more Veggie Broth
- 1 dried bay leaf
- 1½ teaspoons dried oregano leaves
- 1 teaspoon dried basil leaves
- 1 teaspoon salt
- ¼ teaspoon freshly ground black pepper

Seasonal Substitute Only in the summer, use your home-grown or farmers' market fresh tomatoes in place of the canned crushed and diced tomatoes. Blanch 10 to 12 large tomatoes in some boiling water so you can peel them easily. Cut the peeled tomatoes into chunks, and use as directed in the recipe.

BOLOGNESE SAUCE

MAKES 10 CUPS • PREP TIME: 15 MINUTES, PLUS 15 MINUTES TO SOAK
COOK TIME: 8 TO 9 HOURS ON LOW

Traditional Bolognese sauce is made with beef and pork, but this vegetarian version is equally hearty, with a rich, deep flavor. Lots of mushrooms add meaty flavor and texture. Serve over hot cooked pasta for a wonderful, comforting meal.

1. In a small bowl, cover the porcini mushrooms with the warm water. Let stand for 15 minutes.

2. Drain the mushrooms, reserving the soaking liquid. Strain the mushroom liquid through cheesecloth to remove any grit. Remove and discard the mushroom stems, and chop the tops.

3. In a 4- or 5-quart slow cooker, stir well to combine the porcini mushrooms, mushroom soaking liquid, cremini and shiitake mushrooms, onions, carrots, crushed tomatoes, tomato paste, tamari, salt, oregano, and basil.

4. Cover and cook on low for 8 to 9 hours, or until the sauce is thickened.

5. Cool at room temperature for 30 minutes, and then refrigerate for up to 1 week in an airtight container. Freeze for longer storage.

2 ounces dried porcini mushrooms

1 cup warm water

2 cups chopped cremini mushrooms

1 cup chopped shiitake mushrooms

2 onions, finely chopped

2 carrots, chopped

2 (28-ounce) cans crushed tomatoes

3 tablespoons tomato paste

2 tablespoons tamari

1 teaspoon salt

1 teaspoon dried oregano leaves

1 teaspoon dried basil leaves

Ingredient Tip Tamari is used here as a gluten-free alternative to soy sauce. Though many brands of tamari are completely gluten-free, it's important for those with celiac disease or gluten allergies to check the label before using.

SPRING VEGETABLE BROTH

MAKES 10 CUPS • PREP TIME: 20 MINUTES • COOK TIME: 6 TO 8 HOURS ON LOW

Spring vegetables make a light and refreshing broth that is delicious used in soups such as pea soup or asparagus soup. Like all broths, it freezes very well. Be sure to make this broth while your herbs are still fresh and flavorful.

- 1 onion, chopped
- 6 green onions, chopped
- 1 fennel bulb, trimmed and chopped
- 2 leeks, chopped
- 4 celery stalks, sliced
- 3 fresh thyme sprigs
- ⅓ cup chopped fresh flat-leaf parsley
- ¼ cup chopped fresh basil leaves
- 1 teaspoon salt
- 9 cups water

1. In a 4- or 5-quart slow cooker, stir well to combine the onion, green onions, fennel, leeks, celery, thyme, parsley, basil, salt, and water.

2. Cover and cook on low for 6 to 8 hours.

3. Strain the broth into a large container, discarding the solids, and then cool at room temperature for 30 minutes.

4. Refrigerate for up to 1 week in an airtight container, or freeze for longer storage.

Seasonal Substitute

In the spring and summer, add some artichokes, carrot tops, spring onions, or pea greens to this broth for more flavor.

FRESH TOMATO-BASIL SAUCE

MAKES 10 CUPS • PREP TIME: 25 MINUTES • COOK TIME: 6 HOURS ON LOW, PLUS 2 HOURS ON HIGH

This wonderful sauce can be made with winter tomatoes because the flavor concentrates as the sauce cooks. But it is wonderful in the summer, with tomatoes just picked from the garden or purchased from your local farmers' market. It's all about the basil, and both fresh and dried are used.

8 cups chopped fresh tomatoes (10 to 12 tomatoes)

¼ cup extra-virgin olive oil

1 onion, finely chopped

2 shallots, minced

2 garlic cloves, minced

1 tablespoon honey

1½ teaspoons dried basil leaves

1 teaspoon salt

⅛ teaspoon freshly ground black pepper

½ cup whole basil leaves on the stem

1. In a 4-quart slow cooker, stir well to combine the tomatoes, olive oil, onion, shallots, garlic, honey, basil, salt, and pepper.

2. Cover and cook on low for 6 hours.

3. Stir, add the fresh basil, and stir again. Cover and cook on high for another 2 hours.

4. Remove the basil with tongs and discard.

5. This sauce can be used as is, or you can purée it with an immersion blender right in the slow cooker.

6. Refrigerate leftover sauce in an airtight container for up to 3 days, or freeze for longer storage.

PRIMAVERA PASTA SAUCE

MAKES 8 CUPS • PREP TIME: 20 MINUTES • COOK TIME: 6 TO 8 HOURS ON LOW

Primavera is the Italian word for spring, the season when many of the ingredients in this colorful sauce are readily available. This sauce is usually made with broccoli and peas, but those ingredients don't cook well in the slow cooker. In this recipe, carrots and bell peppers add a fresh pop.

1. In a 4- or 5-quart slow cooker, stir well to combine the crushed tomatoes, tomato paste, carrots, red bell peppers, zucchini, onion, garlic, Veggie Broth, oregano, basil, salt, and pepper.

2. Cover and cook on low for 6 to 8 hours, or until the sauce is thickened.

3. You can leave this sauce slightly chunky, or purée it right in the slow cooker using an immersion blender or potato masher.

4. Cool and refrigerate in an airtight container up to 3 days, or freeze for longer storage.

1 (28-ounce) can crushed tomatoes in purée

1 (6-ounce) can tomato paste

3 carrots, sliced

2 red bell peppers, seeded and chopped

1 zucchini, peeled and cubed

1 onion, chopped

5 garlic cloves, sliced

2 cups Veggie Broth (page 60)

1 teaspoon dried oregano leaves

1 teaspoon dried basil leaves

1 teaspoon salt

⅛ teaspoon freshly ground black pepper

The Next Day Whenever you freeze anything, especially a sauce that may be difficult to identify, make sure you mark the container holding the food with the name of the recipe and the date it was made. Sauces can be frozen for up to 4 to 5 months. To use, defrost in the fridge overnight, heat, and serve.

PUMPKIN BUTTER

MAKES 5 CUPS • PREP TIME: 10 MINUTES • COOK TIME: 5 TO 6 HOURS ON LOW

Pumpkin butter is a wonderful condiment that can be used in place of butter on toast, pancakes, or waffles. It is rich, thick, and a deep brown color, with a tasty autumn flavor of cinnamon and nutmeg. This recipe does need to be stirred occasionally to prevent burning. Make it on a cold winter day when you're at home puttering around the kitchen.

1. In a 2-quart slow cooker, stir well to combine the pumpkin, brown sugar, sugar, honey, ginger root, lemon juice, cinnamon, nutmeg, ground ginger, cardamom, allspice, and salt.

2. Cover and cook on low for 5 to 6 hours, stirring every hour so the mixture doesn't burn, until the pumpkin butter is rich, dark golden brown, and thick.

3. Stir again, and spoon into containers. Let cool for 30 minutes at room temperature, cover tightly, and refrigerate for up to 1 week. Freeze for longer storage.

2 (15-ounce) cans solid pack pumpkin

1 cup brown sugar

½ cup sugar

¼ cup honey

2 tablespoons grated fresh ginger root

2 tablespoons freshly squeezed lemon juice

2 teaspoons ground cinnamon

1 teaspoon ground nutmeg

1 teaspoon ground ginger

½ teaspoon ground cardamom

¼ teaspoon ground allspice

½ teaspoon salt

Seasonal Substitute When sugar pumpkins, those little sweet fruits, are in season, use them in place of the canned pumpkin. Peel two or three of the pumpkins, remove the seeds, and cut the flesh into cubes. Add another 2 hours of cooking time to the recipe, but still remember to stir it occasionally.

APPLE-PEAR BUTTER

MAKES 6 CUPS • PREP TIME: 25 MINUTES • COOK TIME: 8 HOURS TO 9 HOURS, 20 MINUTES ON LOW

Apple-pear butter is the best of both worlds. When cooked with spices and some maple syrup and maple sugar, this delicious condiment captures the flavors of fall. Nothing beats a breakfast of a thick slice of whole-grain toast with a generous spread of this butter on it on the first crisp mornings of fall.

1. In a 3- or 4-quart slow cooker, stir well to combine the apples, pears, brown sugar, maple syrup, maple sugar, lemon juice, cinnamon, nutmeg, and salt.

2. Cover and cook on low for 8 to 9 hours, stirring occasionally if you are at home.

3. Stir again, and then stir in the vanilla. Taste the butter to see if it needs more sugar. If it does, add some and cook for another 20 minutes on low.

4. Stir the butter again, and portion it into containers. Cool at room temperature for 20 to 30 minutes, tightly cover, and refrigerate for up to 1 week. You can freeze this butter for longer storage, too.

5 apples, peeled, cored, and cubed

4 pears, peeled, cored, and cubed

½ cup brown sugar, plus more if needed

⅓ cup maple syrup

¼ cup maple sugar, plus more if needed

1 tablespoon freshly squeezed lemon juice

2 teaspoons ground cinnamon

¼ teaspoon ground nutmeg

¼ teaspoon salt

2 teaspoons vanilla

Prep It Right

Fill your slow cooker about three-quarters full for this and other recipes that cook down, such as applesauce. Add or subtract the amount of fruit to fit your slow cooker.

CARAMELIZED ONION-TOMATO SAUCE

MAKES 12 CUPS • PREP TIME: 10 MINUTES • COOK TIME: 8 TO 10 HOURS ON LOW

Caramelized onions add wonderful, robust flavor to this spicy tomato sauce. You do need to make Caramelized Onions (page 181) in order to give this sauce the proper flavor, but it is well worth the time. Of course, that recipe makes so much it only makes sense to transform some into this sauce.

1. In a 4- to 5-quart slow cooker, stir well to combine the Caramelized Onions, onions, crushed tomatoes, tomato sauce, tomato paste, oregano, basil, thyme, salt, and pepper.

2. Cover and cook on low for 8 to 10 hours, or until the sauce is thickened and bubbly.

3. Taste for seasoning, and adjust as needed. Cool the sauce at room temperature for 30 minutes.

4. Refrigerate in airtight containers for up to 1 week, or freeze for longer storage.

2 cups Caramelized Onions (page 181)

2 onions, chopped

2 (28-ounce) cans crushed tomatoes in purée

2 (8-ounce) cans tomato sauce

1 (6-ounce) can tomato paste

2 teaspoons dried oregano leaves

2 teaspoons dried basil leaves

2 teaspoons dried thyme leaves

2 teaspoons salt

½ teaspoon freshly ground black pepper

SPICY GREEN SAUCE

MAKES 8 CUPS • PREP TIME: 25 MINUTES • COOK TIME: 7 TO 9 HOURS ON LOW

Green sauce, or salsa verde, is made from tomatillos and peppers—poblano, habanero, jalapeño, and green bell. I use it as a condiment with just about any type of Mexican dish, or add it to cooked vegetables and beans to make great tacos or enchiladas.

1. In a 4- or 5-quart slow cooker, stir well to combine the tomatillos, poblanos, green bell peppers, onions, jalapeños, habanero, garlic, Veggie Broth, salt, coriander, cumin, black pepper, and cayenne pepper.

2. Cover and cook on low for 7 to 9 hours, or until the tomatillos and peppers are soft.

3. Mash the vegetables right in the slow cooker using a potato masher or an immersion blender. Stir in the cilantro.

4. Let the sauce cool for 20 to 30 minutes, and refrigerate in airtight containers for up to 1 week, or freeze for longer storage.

2 pounds tomatillos, husks removed

4 poblano peppers, seeded and chopped

3 green bell peppers, seeded and chopped

2 onions, chopped

3 jalapeño peppers, chopped

1 habanero pepper, chopped

5 garlic cloves, minced

3 cups Veggie Broth (page 60)

1 teaspoon salt

1 teaspoon dried coriander

1 teaspoon ground cumin

¼ teaspoon freshly ground black pepper

¼ teaspoon ground cayenne pepper

¼ cup minced fresh cilantro

TEX-MEX PASTA SAUCE

MAKES 10 CUPS • PREP TIME: 20 MINUTES • COOK TIME: 6 TO 8 HOURS ON LOW

This sauce is alive with the flavors of Tex-Mex cuisine, a fusion of Texas culture and Mexican food. I like this as a twist on the more familiar Italian pasta sauce. It's unexpected and a treat for your taste buds. You can make this sauce as spicy or as mild as you'd like by adjusting the amount of peppers you use.

1. In a 4- or 5-quart slow cooker, stir well to combine the crushed tomatoes, diced tomatoes, tomato paste, onions, garlic, poblanos, jalapeños, habanero, Veggie Broth, chili powder, cumin, oregano, salt, black pepper, and red pepper flakes.

2. Cover and cook on low for 6 to 8 hours, or until the sauce is thickened.

3. You can leave this sauce slightly chunky, or purée it right in the slow cooker using an immersion blender or potato masher.

4. Cool and refrigerate in an airtight container up to 3 days, or freeze for longer storage.

Seasonal Substitute

Nothing beats the taste of fresh summer tomatoes; use 6 to 7 cups seeded and chopped tomatoes in place of the canned crushed and diced tomatoes. But use the tomato paste; it's necessary to add depth of flavor.

1 (28-ounce) can crushed tomatoes in purée

1 (14-ounce) can diced tomatoes, undrained

1 (6-ounce) can tomato paste

2 onions, chopped

4 garlic cloves, minced

2 poblano peppers, seeded and chopped

3 jalapeño peppers, seeded and minced

1 habanero pepper, seeded and minced

2 cups Veggie Broth (page 60)

1 tablespoon chili powder

1 teaspoon ground cumin

1 teaspoon dried oregano leaves

1 teaspoon salt

¼ teaspoon freshly ground black pepper

¼ teaspoon crushed red pepper flakes

SALTED ALMOND-CARAMEL SAUCE

MAKES 4 CUPS • PREP TIME: 10 MINUTES • COOK TIME: 8 TO 9 HOURS ON LOW

Salted caramel sauce is a trendy flavor—but the best kind of trend. It's delicious on everything from ice cream to pound cake to rice pudding. I use it in several recipes in the Desserts and Breads chapters of this book. But did you know you can make this sweet sauce in the slow cooker? You can, and you won't be sorry about it one bit.

2 (14-ounce) cans sweetened condensed milk

¼ cup almond butter

¼ cup almond milk

1 teaspoon salt

¼ cup amaretto liqueur (optional) or more almond milk

4 teaspoons vanilla, divided

1. In a large bowl, whisk together the condensed milk, almond butter, almond milk, salt, and amaretto liqueur (if using) until smooth.

2. Pour half of the mixture into each of 2 pint-size heatproof canning jars with lids. Make sure there is at least ½ inch of headspace in the jars. Seal them tightly.

3. Place the jars in a 4-quart slow cooker, and pour in enough water so the jars are completely covered with 1 inch of water above the jars.

4. Cover and cook on low for 8 to 9 hours.

5. Turn off the slow cooker, and carefully remove the hot jars from the water using tongs. Set them on a wire rack to cool. Once they are cool enough to remove the lids, stir 2 teaspoons of vanilla into each jar.

6. Cover tightly again and refrigerate for up to 3 months. Use some sauce in a recipe, or heat in the microwave and drizzle over your favorite dessert.

SOUPS & STEWS

CREAMY BROCCOLI SOUP

SERVES: 6 • PREP TIME: 20 MINUTES • COOK TIME: 7½ TO 8½ HOURS ON LOW

Broccoli makes a velvety, delectable soup when puréed with cream. The key to slow cooker broccoli soup is to slow cook the stems first, then purée, and the florets are added and cooked just long enough to heat them.

1. Wash the broccoli and cut the florets off the stems and set them aside. Cut the stems into 2-inch pieces.

2. In a 4-quart slow cooker, stir well to combine the broccoli stems, onion, celery, garlic, Veggie Broth, salt, thyme, and pepper.

3. Cover and cook on low for 7 to 8 hours, or until the vegetables are very tender.

4. Purée the soup right in the slow cooker with an immersion blender, or transfer the soup, working in batches if necessary, to a food processor or blender and blend until smooth (and return the soup to the slow cooker).

5. Stir in the cream and the broccoli florets.

6. Cover and cook on low for 20 to 30 minutes, or until the soup is hot and the florets are tender.

7. Stir gently and serve.

1½ pounds fresh broccoli

1 onion, chopped

3 celery stalks, sliced

4 garlic cloves, sliced

4 cups Veggie Broth (page 60)

1 teaspoon salt

1 teaspoon dried thyme leaves

⅛ teaspoon freshly ground black pepper

1½ cups light cream

Perfect Pair Up the comfort level of this soup and serve it with hot cornbread right out of the oven. You can use a mix and stir in some frozen or fresh corn kernels to add more flavor and nutrition, or bake it from scratch. Try it with the Tex-Mex Cornbread (page 240) for a little kick.

CREAMY TOMATO BISQUE

SERVES: 6 TO 8 • PREP TIME: 15 MINUTES • COOK TIME: 7 ½ TO 8 ½ HOURS ON LOW

"Bisque" is simply a smooth soup that has some cream added. It is traditionally made from shellfish, but the term can refer to any creamy, puréed soup. This soup is delicious, whether you make it from canned tomatoes or tomatoes fresh from your garden.

1. In a 4-quart slow cooker, stir well to combine the crushed tomatoes, tomato sauce, tomato paste, shallots, garlic, Veggie Broth, butter, salt, pepper, bay leaf, thyme, and marjoram.

2. Cover and cook on low for 7 to 8 hours. Remove and discard the bay leaf.

3. Purée the soup right in the slow cooker, using an immersion blender. You can also transfer the soup, in batches if needed, to a food processor or blender and blend until smooth (and return it to the slow cooker).

4. Stir in the cream and Parmesan cheese.

5. Cover and cook on low for another 20 to 25 minutes, or until the soup is hot.

6. Stir gently and serve.

- 1 (28-ounce) can crushed tomatoes in purée
- 1 (8-ounce) can tomato sauce
- 3 tablespoons tomato paste
- 2 shallots, minced
- 1 garlic clove, minced
- 3 cups Veggie Broth (page 60)
- 2 tablespoons butter
- 1 teaspoon salt
- ⅛ teaspoon freshly ground black pepper
- 1 dried bay leaf
- 1 teaspoon dried thyme leaves
- 1 teaspoon dried marjoram leaves
- 1 cup heavy (whipping) cream
- 1 cup grated Parmesan cheese

Seasonal Substitute

When fresh, ripe, red tomatoes are in season, use them instead of the canned tomatoes in this recipe. Use about 2 ½ pounds of tomatoes, seeded and roughly chopped.

CORN-WILD RICE CHOWDER

SERVES: 6 • PREP TIME: 20 MINUTES
COOK TIME: 8 HOURS, 15 MINUTES TO 9 HOURS, 20 MINUTES ON LOW

A "chowder" is somewhere between a soup and a stew. It is thick with chunks of vegetables, and it (almost) always has some dairy added. It makes a really good supper on a cold winter night—nothing warms the heart and stomach better.

1. In a 4-quart slow cooker, stir well to combine the wild rice, potatoes, onion, garlic, celery, red bell peppers, carrots, corn, Veggie Broth, salt, pepper, and thyme.

2. Cover and cook on low for 8 to 9 hours, or until the rice and vegetables are tender.

3. At this point you can purée part of the chowder to help thicken it. Remove a cup or two from the slow cooker, and purée in a food processor, blender, or with an immersion blender. Return it to the chowder.

4. In a small bowl, mix well to combine the cornstarch and light cream until no lumps of cornstarch remain. Stir the cornstarch mixture into the chowder.

5. Cover and cook on low for another 15 to 20 minutes, or until the chowder is thickened to your preferred consistency, and serve.

1 cup wild rice

3 Yukon Gold potatoes, peeled and cubed

1 onion, chopped

3 garlic cloves, minced

4 celery stalks, sliced

2 red bell peppers, seeded and chopped

3 carrots, sliced

2 cups frozen corn

5 cups Veggie Broth (page 60)

1 teaspoon salt

⅛ teaspoon freshly ground black pepper

1 teaspoon dried thyme leaves

2 tablespoons cornstarch

1 cup light cream

Seasonal Substitute Fresh summer corn tastes like no other. To use in this chowder, cut the kernels off the cobs, cover, and refrigerate. Scrape the cobs with the back of a knife, and put this creamy extra in with the wild rice and other ingredients. Slow cook the chowder according to the recipe. When you add the cream mixture, stir in the fresh corn and cook until hot.

CHEESY VEGETABLE SOUP

SERVES: 8 • PREP TIME: 25 MINUTES
COOK TIME: 8 HOURS, 10 MINUTES TO 9 HOURS, 15 MINUTES ON LOW

It's all about the cheese, and you can use your favorite cheese in this hearty and warming recipe. I like Cheddar or Colby myself. And you can mix up the vegetables, too. That's one of the nicest things about soups: They are very tolerant, which means you can make lots of changes and the recipe will still be wonderful.

1. In a 4- or 5-quart slow cooker, stir well to combine the onion, garlic, mushrooms, carrots, parsnip, Veggie Broth, marjoram, rosemary, bay leaf, salt, and pepper.

2. Cover and cook on low for 8 to 9 hours, or until the vegetables are tender.

3. Stir in the cream.

4. In a medium bowl, toss the cheese with the flour, and add the mixture to the slow cooker, stirring.

5. Cover and cook on low for 10 to 15 minutes, or until the cheese is melted and the soup is slightly thickened.

6. Stir gently and serve.

1 onion, chopped

3 garlic cloves, minced

2 cups sliced mushrooms

4 carrots, sliced

1 parsnip, peeled and sliced

6 cups Veggie Broth (page 60)

1 teaspoon dried marjoram leaves

1 sprig fresh rosemary

1 dried bay leaf

1 teaspoon salt

⅛ teaspoon freshly ground black pepper

1 cup light cream or whole milk

2 cups shredded Colby or Cheddar cheese

2 tablespoons all-purpose flour

PASTA *e* FAGIOLI

SERVES: 6 • PREP TIME: 20 MINUTES
COOK TIME: 8 TO 9 HOURS ON LOW, PLUS 15 TO 25 MINUTES ON HIGH

Pasta e Fagioli, *usually called by the slang term "pasta fazool," is a soup rich with vegetables, legumes, and pasta. It's a meal in one bowl, really. A rind of Parmesan cheese is necessary to the flavor of this soup, but if you can't find it, add some extra grated cheese at the end of cooking time.*

1. In a 4- or 5-quart slow cooker, stir well to combine the Spicy Pinto Beans, onion, garlic, carrots, celery, Veggie Broth, diced tomatoes, tomato paste, honey, bay leaf, cheese rind, thyme, salt, and pepper.

2. Cover and cook on low for 8 to 9 hours, or until the vegetables are tender. Remove and discard the Parmesan rind and the bay leaf.

3. Transfer 1 cup of the soup from the slow cooker to a food processor or blender to purée. Stir the purée into the soup.

4. Add the pasta to the soup, and stir.

5. Cover and cook on high for another 15 to 25 minutes, or until the pasta is tender.

6. Stir the Parmesan cheese into the soup and serve.

- 2 cups cooked Spicy Pinto Beans (page 28) or 1 (16-ounce) can pinto beans, drained and rinsed
- 1 onion, chopped
- 3 garlic cloves, minced
- 3 carrots, sliced
- 3 celery stalks, sliced
- 6 cups Veggie Broth (page 60)
- 1 (14-ounce) can diced tomatoes, undrained
- ¼ cup tomato paste
- 1 tablespoon honey
- 1 dried bay leaf
- 1 Parmesan cheese rind
- 1 teaspoon dried thyme leaves
- 1 teaspoon salt
- ⅛ teaspoon freshly ground black pepper
- 1 cup small shell pasta
- ½ cup grated Parmesan cheese, for garnish

Perfect Pair This soup begs to be served with garlic toast. To make, slice crusty French bread into 1-inch-thick slices. Spread with a mixture of softened butter, minced garlic, and olive oil. Place on a baking sheet, and place under a preheated broiler until the butter bubbles and the bread is brown.

MUSHROOM-BARLEY STEW

SERVES: 6 • PREP TIME: 20 MINUTES, PLUS 30 MINUTES TO SOAK
COOK TIME: 7 HOURS, 10 MINUTES TO 9 HOURS, 15 MINUTES

Barley is the perfect grain for soup. It adds wonderful texture to the soup and is loaded with fiber and minerals such as manganese, selenium, and magnesium. Mushrooms and barley go hand-in-hand. This hearty soup features three kinds of mushrooms for rich, satisfying, complex flavors.

1. In a small bowl, cover the dried shiitake mushrooms with the hot water and let stand for 30 minutes. Strain the mushrooms, reserving the soaking liquid. Strain the liquid through cheesecloth to remove any grit.

2. In a 4- or 5-quart slow cooker, stir well to combine the shiitakes, the soaking liquid, and the button and cremini mushrooms, carrots, barley, onion, garlic, Veggie Broth, marjoram, salt, and pepper.

3. Cover and cook on low for 7 to 9 hours, or until the barley is tender.

4. Stir in the spinach, cover, and cook on low for another 10 to 15 minutes, or until the spinach is wilted.

5. Stir gently and serve.

1 ounce dried shiitake mushrooms

1 cup hot water

2 cups sliced button mushrooms

2 cups sliced cremini mushrooms

3 carrots, sliced

1 cup hulled barley

1 onion, chopped

4 garlic cloves, minced

5 cups Veggie Broth (page 60)

1 teaspoon dried marjoram leaves

1 teaspoon salt

⅛ teaspoon freshly ground black pepper

3 cups baby spinach leaves

MINESTRONE

SERVES: 8 • PREP TIME: 25 MINUTES
COOK TIME: 8 HOURS, 15 MINUTES TO 10 HOURS, 20 MINUTES ON LOW

Minestrone is a classic Italian vegetable soup. It's rich and flavorful and should be in everyone's repertoire; it's definitely one of my go-to soups. You can use just about any vegetable you can think of in minestrone. As with all slow cooker soups that call for pasta, it should be added in at the end of the cooking time.

1. In a 5-quart slow cooker, stir well to combine the onion, garlic, celery, carrots, mushrooms, beans, crushed tomatoes, diced tomatoes, tomato paste, Veggie Broth, oregano, basil, thyme, salt, and pepper.

2. Cover and cook on low for 8 to 10 hours, or until the vegetables are tender.

3. Stir in the pasta and spinach leaves.

4. Cover and cook on low for another 15 to 20 minutes, or until the pasta is tender.

5. Stir in the Parmesan cheese and serve.

Perfect Pair Crisply toasted cheesy garlic bread is a great pair with this recipe. To make, slice a loaf of crusty French bread into 1-inch slices, but don't cut all the way through the loaf. Combine 2 tablespoons olive oil with 3 minced garlic cloves, and drizzle on the loaf, making sure to get some in between the bread slices. Wrap in aluminum foil, and bake in a 400°F oven for 20 minutes. Unwrap and top the loaf with 2 cups shredded mozzarella cheese. Bake for another 5 to 10 minutes and serve.

1 onion, chopped

5 garlic cloves, minced

3 celery stalks, sliced

2 carrots, sliced

1 cup sliced cremini mushrooms

1 (14-ounce) can cannellini beans, rinsed and drained

1 (28-ounce) can crushed tomatoes in purée

1 (14-ounce) can diced tomatoes, undrained

3 tablespoons tomato paste

4 cups Veggie Broth (page 60)

1 teaspoon dried oregano leaves

1 teaspoon dried basil leaves

1 teaspoon dried thyme leaves

1 teaspoon salt

⅛ teaspoon freshly ground black pepper

1 cup small shell pasta

2 cups baby spinach leaves

½ cup grated Parmesan cheese

CURRIED CARROT SOUP

SERVES: 6 • PREP TIME: 25 MINUTES • COOK TIME: 7½ TO 9½ HOURS ON LOW

If you haven't already tried—and fallen in love with—carrot soup, get ready. It is velvety and flavorful, especially when made with curry powder. This soup is good hot or cold. To serve it cold, chill for a few hours, and serve with a dollop of sour cream and a sprinkle of toasted pine nuts on top.

7 large carrots, sliced

1 onion, finely chopped

1 leek, chopped

2 garlic cloves, minced

6 cups Veggie Broth (page 60)

2 tablespoons honey

1 tablespoon freshly squeezed lemon juice

1 tablespoon curry powder

½ teaspoon ground ginger

1 teaspoon salt

⅛ teaspoon freshly ground black pepper

½ cup almond milk

1. In a 4- or 5-quart slow cooker, stir well to combine the carrots onion, leek, garlic, Veggie Broth, honey, lemon juice, curry powder, ginger, salt, and pepper.

2. Cover and cook on low for 7 to 9 hours, or until the carrots are very tender.

3. Stir in the almond milk.

4. Purée the soup right in the slow cooker using an immersion blender, or purée it in batches in a food processor or blender, and then return the soup to the slow cooker.

5. Cook the soup on low for another 20 minutes or so, until heated through.

6. Stir gently and serve.

When you purée hot liquids in a food processor or blender, you have to do it in small batches because hot liquid expands in those appliances. Fill the food processor or blender no more than three-quarters full. Cover the lid with a folded towel, and hold it down so the soup doesn't spurt out. As you finish puréeing each batch, return it to the slow cooker.

VEGETARIAN SCOTCH BROTH

SERVES: 6 • PREP TIME: 20 MINUTES • COOK TIME: 7 TO 9 HOURS ON LOW

Scotch broth is much heartier than it sounds. Traditionally, it is a barley vegetable soup made with beef broth and lamb. But because barley and vegetables are the most important ingredients, it's easy to skip the beef and lamb and go full vegetarian without missing a beat.

1 onion, chopped

1 leek, chopped

3 carrots, sliced

1 parsnip, peeled and cubed

2 cups chopped green cabbage

1 cup hulled barley

7 cups Veggie Broth (page 60)

1 teaspoon dried thyme leaves

1 teaspoon dried marjoram leaves

1 teaspoon salt

⅛ teaspoon freshly ground black pepper

1. In a 4- or 5-quart slow cooker, stir well to combine the onion, leek, carrots, parsnip, cabbage, barley, Veggie Broth, thyme, marjoram, salt, and pepper.

2. Cover and cook on low for 7 to 9 hours, or until the barley and vegetables are tender.

3. Stir gently and serve.

SPLIT PEA SOUP

SERVES: 6 • PREP TIME: 20 MINUTES • COOK TIME: 8 TO 10 HOURS ON LOW

Split peas don't take very long to cook. They are great for the slow cooker, though, because when they are cooked for a long time, they break down into a creamy emulsion that has the best texture, and they help thicken the soup. I like using caramelized onions and mushrooms for extra flavor.

1 pound dried split peas

2 cups Caramelized Onions (page 181)

3 carrots, sliced

3 celery stalks, sliced

1½ cups sliced cremini mushrooms

1 Yukon Gold potato, peeled and chopped

3 garlic cloves, sliced

6 cups Veggie Broth (page 60)

1 fresh rosemary sprig

1 teaspoon dried marjoram leaves

1 teaspoon salt

⅛ teaspoon freshly ground black pepper

1. Sort the split peas, rinse well, and drain.

2. In a 4- or 5-quart slow cooker, stir well to combine the split peas, Caramelized Onions, carrots, celery, mushrooms, potato, garlic, Veggie Broth, rosemary, marjoram, salt, and pepper.

3. Cover and cook on low for 8 to 10 hours, or until the peas are very soft and all the vegetables are tender.

4. Remove and discard the rosemary stem, stir well, and serve.

Perfect Pair

A crisp green salad is the ideal accompaniment to this rich and smooth soup. Some textural contrast is always good in a meal. Toss fresh romaine with chopped avocados and cherry tomatoes, and drizzle with an Italian salad dressing.

BLACK BEAN SOUP

SERVES: 6 • PREP TIME: 20 MINUTES, PLUS OVERNIGHT TO SOAK
COOK TIME: 8 HOURS, 20 MINUTES TO 10 HOURS, 20 MINUTES ON LOW

Black beans are fabulous in soups. This recipe is simple, but full of texture and flavor. Bonus: It's inexpensive and healthy—full of fiber, calcium, iron, and other important minerals. Mild, spicy, or somewhere in between, make it according to your taste.

1. Sort the beans, rinse well, and drain. In a 4- or 5-quart slow cooker, cover the beans with cool water. Let stand overnight.

2. In the morning, drain the beans, discarding the soaking liquid. In the slow cooker, stir well to combine the beans, onion, garlic, jalapeño, carrots, tomatoes, Veggie Broth, oregano, salt, and pepper.

3. Cover and cook on low for 8 to 10 hours, or until the beans are tender.

4. Transfer a cup of the soup to a blender or food processor, and purée. Return the purée to the slow cooker.

5. Cover and cook on low for another 20 minutes.

6. Stir, ladle into bowls, garnish each with the cilantro, and serve.

2 cups dried black beans, sorted and rinsed

1 onion, chopped

3 garlic cloves, minced

1 jalapeño pepper, minced

4 carrots, sliced

1 (14-ounce) can diced tomatoes, undrained

6 cups Veggie Broth (page 60)

1 teaspoon dried oregano leaves

1 teaspoon salt

⅛ teaspoon freshly ground black pepper

⅓ cup chopped fresh cilantro

Perfect Pair This soup can be garnished with any number of different ingredients for added texture and contrast. Try sour cream, shredded cheese, chopped avocados, or salsa.

BEER-CHEESE SOUP

SERVES: 6 TO 8 • PREP TIME: 20 MINUTES
COOK TIME: 7 HOURS, 10 MINUTES TO 9 HOURS, 15 MINUTES ON LOW

Beer-cheese soup is a classic and perfect for the slow cooker. The mellow, slightly nutty flavor of beer pairs so well with melted cheese. This is really a meal, so don't serve it as part of a larger menu; you'll just end up with leftovers of everything else after this soup fills you up!

1. In a medium microwave-safe bowl, microwave the butter and onion on high for 1 minute. Stir, and microwave on high for another minute, or until the onion is crisp-tender.

2. In a 4- or 5-quart slow cooker, stir well to combine the onion mixture, garlic, carrots, celery, Veggie Broth, beer, salt, and pepper.

3. Cover and cook on low for 7 to 9 hours, or until the vegetables are very tender.

4. In a large bowl, toss the Cheddar and Havarti cheeses with the cornstarch, and add to the slow cooker. Stir well.

5. In a small bowl, stir to combine the tamari, mustard, and cream. Add to the slow cooker, and stir well.

6. Cover and cook on low for another 10 to 15 minutes, or until the cheese is melted and the soup is slightly thickened.

7. Stir gently and serve.

- 3 tablespoons butter
- 2 onions, chopped
- 5 garlic cloves, minced
- 3 carrots, sliced
- 2 celery stalks, sliced
- 4 cups Veggie Broth (page 60)
- 1 (12-ounce) bottle mild beer, such as a lager
- ½ teaspoon salt
- ⅛ teaspoon freshly ground black pepper
- 2 cups shredded Cheddar cheese
- 1 cup shredded Havarti cheese
- 3 tablespoons cornstarch
- 1 tablespoon tamari
- 1 tablespoon Dijon mustard
- 1 cup light cream

Perfect Pair This soup can be garnished with popcorn on top—yes, popcorn! For even more flavor, use cheese-covered popcorn. Pop some corn, and then toss with grated Parmesan cheese.

FRENCH ONION SOUP

SERVES: 6 • PREP TIME: 20 MINUTES • COOK TIME: 8 TO 10 HOURS ON LOW

A rich vegetable broth, caramelized onions, and freshly chopped onions give this soup a wonderful, satisfying depth of flavor. To serve this in the traditional way, top it with cheese bread. Just be careful, because it is very hot.

2 cups Caramelized Onions (page 181)

2 onions, chopped

6 garlic cloves, sliced

6 cups Roasted Root Vegetable Broth (page 61) or Veggie Broth (page 60)

1 tablespoon tamari

1 tablespoon freshly squeezed lemon juice

2 fresh thyme sprigs

1 teaspoon salt

⅛ teaspoon freshly ground black pepper

1. In a 4-quart slow cooker, combine the Caramelized Onions, chopped onions, garlic, Roasted Root Vegetable Broth, tamari, lemon juice, thyme, salt, and pepper.

2. Cover and cook on low for 8 to 10 hours, or until the onions are very tender.

3. Remove the thyme stems, stir gently, and serve.

Perfect Pair This soup is traditionally topped with toasted bread and melted cheese. Ladle the soup into 6 individual oven-proof ceramic bowls, and place them on a sturdy baking sheet or sheets. Toast 6 slices of French bread, and top each with ⅓ cup shredded Gruyère cheese. Put the bread on the soup, and place the baking sheet under a preheated broiler for 2 to 4 minutes, or until the cheese starts to brown.

ITALIAN TORTELLINI SOUP

SERVES: 6 • PREP TIME: 20 MINUTES
COOK TIME: 8 HOURS, 10 MINUTES TO 9 HOURS, 15 MINUTES ON LOW

Tortellini is a small, ring-shaped pasta stuffed with cheese or meat. It's delicious in a soup packed full of lots of different vegetables. Serve this recipe with some freshly grated Parmesan cheese, garlic toast, and a side salad—well, dinner's ready.

1. In a 4- or 5-quart slow cooker, stir well to combine the onion, garlic, carrots, fennel, diced tomatoes, tomato sauce, Veggie Broth, Italian seasoning, basil, salt, and pepper.

2. Cover and cook on low for 8 to 9 hours, or until the vegetables are tender.

3. Add the frozen cheese tortellini and stir.

4. Cover and cook on low for another 10 to 15 minutes, or until the tortellini is tender.

5. Stir gently, ladle the soup into bowls, garnish with the cheese, and serve.

1 onion, chopped

3 garlic cloves, minced

3 carrots, sliced

1 cup chopped fennel bulb

1 (14-ounce) can diced
   tomatoes, undrained

1 (8-ounce) can
   tomato sauce

5 cups Veggie Broth
   (page 60)

1 teaspoon dried Italian
   seasoning

1 teaspoon dried basil leaves

½ teaspoon salt

⅛ teaspoon freshly ground
   black pepper

1 (20-ounce) package frozen
   cheese tortellini

½ cup grated
   Parmesan cheese

Prep It Right

Frozen tortellini are precooked, so you are really just thawing them in the slow cooker. You can use dried tortellini, too; the cooking time in the soup will be longer. Just cook until the tortellini are tender and the filling is hot.

LENTIL *and* CHESTNUT SOUP

SERVES: 6 • PREP TIME: 20 MINUTES, PLUS 10 MINUTES TO SOAK
COOK TIME: 8 TO 9 HOURS ON LOW, PLUS 20 MINUTES ON HIGH

Most people only know chestnuts from Christmas carols, but they are delicious, rich, and add great flavor to this thick and creamy soup. The lentils are cooked until they dissolve, and the chestnuts are added at the end of the cooking time. Make sure you use chestnuts, which are brown and round—don't use water chestnuts! Purée the soup and dig in.

1. In a small bowl, cover the dried mushrooms with the warm water; let stand for 10 minutes. Drain the mushrooms, reserving the soaking liquid. Strain the soaking liquid through cheesecloth to remove any grit.

2. Chop the mushrooms, discarding the stems if they are tough.

3. In a 4- or 5-quart slow cooker, stir well to combine the mushrooms, soaking liquid, lentils, onion, garlic, carrots, cremini mushrooms, Veggie Broth, salt, marjoram, and pepper.

4. Cover and cook on low for 8 to 9 hours, or until the lentils are almost dissolved and the vegetables are tender.

1 ounce dried porcini mushrooms

½ cup warm water

1½ cups green lentils

1 onion, chopped

4 garlic cloves, minced

2 carrots, chopped

1 cup chopped cremini mushrooms

6 cups Veggie Broth (page 60)

1 teaspoon salt

1 teaspoon dried marjoram leaves

⅛ teaspoon freshly ground black pepper

1 (10-ounce) can peeled chestnuts in water, drained

½ cup sour cream, yogurt, or light cream

5. Stir in the chestnuts, crumbling them as you add them to the slow cooker.

6. Cover and cook on high for another 20 minutes.

7. Purée the soup using an immersion blender right in the slow cooker, or in batches in a food processor or blender (and return the soup to the slow cooker).

8. Serve the soup, garnished with some sour cream drizzled on top.

This soup, like all soups, reheats very well, and actually tastes better the next day as the flavors continue to meld together. Reheat leftovers on the stove top, adding more Veggie Broth if necessary for your desired consistency.

TOMATO-VEGGIE CHOWDER

SERVES: 6 • PREP TIME: 25 MINUTES
COOK TIME: 8 HOURS, 10 MINUTES TO 10 HOURS, 15 MINUTES ON LOW

Tomato soup is the classic of classic soups. I've taken it and packed it full of vegetables, turning it into a chowder. You can use any root vegetable you'd like in this soup, including parsnips and rutabagas. Just peel them and cut them into equal-size pieces so they'll all finish cooking at the same time.

1. In a 4- or 5-quart slow cooker, stir well to combine the onion, mushrooms, carrots, sweet potato, potato, tomatoes, Veggie Broth, salt, basil, and pepper.

2. Cover and cook on low for 8 to 10 hours, or until the vegetables are tender.

3. In a small bowl, whisk together the cream and cornstarch until smooth with no lumps.

4. Stir the cream mixture into the soup, cover, and cook on low for another 10 to 15 minutes, or until the soup is thickened.

5. Stir gently and serve.

Seasonal Substitute In summer, when fresh corn is in season, cut off the kernels and add them to this soup along with the light cream. Sweet corn is best when it's just heated, not cooked through. Then top the soup with some chopped fresh basil leaves from your garden.

1 onion, chopped

2 cups sliced button mushrooms

3 carrots, sliced

1 sweet potato, peeled and cubed

3 Yukon Gold potatoes, peeled and cubed

5 beefsteak tomatoes, seeded and chopped

6 cups Veggie Broth (page 60)

1 teaspoon salt

1 teaspoon dried basil leaves

⅛ teaspoon freshly ground black pepper

1 cup light cream

2 tablespoons cornstarch

BORSCHT

SERVES: 6 • PREP TIME: 25 MINUTES • COOK TIME: 8 TO 10 HOURS ON LOW

Borscht is an Eastern European soup made from beets. Beets are naturally sweet, which makes this soup sweet in turn. Add a delicious tart contrast with a dollop of sour cream or crème fraîche. This soup is as delicious on a warm summer evening as it is on the coldest of winter days.

1. In a 5-quart slow cooker, stir well to combine the beets, onions, garlic, sweet potato, Veggie Broth, diced tomatoes, tomato paste, dill seed, dried dill weed, salt, and pepper.

2. Cover and cook on low for 8 to 10 hours, or until the vegetables are very tender.

3. Stir in the lemon juice, lemon zest, and fresh dill weed, and serve.

6 large beets, peeled and chopped

2 onions, chopped

5 garlic cloves, minced

1 large sweet potato, peeled and chopped

5 cups Veggie Broth (page 60)

1 (14-ounce) can diced tomatoes, undrained

3 tablespoons tomato paste

1 teaspoon dried dill seed

1 teaspoon dried dill weed

1 teaspoon salt

⅛ teaspoon freshly ground black pepper

2 tablespoons freshly squeezed lemon juice

1 teaspoon lemon zest

2 tablespoons chopped fresh dill weed

GREEK VEGETABLE STEW

SERVES: 6 TO 8 • PREP TIME: 25 MINUTES
COOK TIME: 8 TO 9 HOURS ON LOW, PLUS 20 TO 30 MINUTES ON HIGH

The alluring flavors of Greek cuisine include lemon, feta cheese, oregano, garlic, and olive oil. Here these wonderful ingredients combine in your slow cooker for a fragrant stew that is simple to make and even more delicious to eat.

1. Sort the lentils, rinse well, and drain. In a 4- or 5-quart slow cooker, stir well to combine the onion, fennel, tomatoes, garlic, Veggie Broth, water, lemon juice, oregano, salt, and pepper.

2. Cover and cook on low for 8 to 9 hours, or until the lentils are very soft and the vegetables are tender.

3. Stir in the green beans, cover, and cook for another 20 to 30 minutes on high.

4. Stir the stew, and ladle it into bowls. Garnish each with the feta cheese and a drizzle of olive oil, and serve.

Prep It Right To seed a tomato, cut the tomato into fourths. Using your fingers, pull out the seeds and the clear pulp. Then chop the tomato and add it to the recipe.

1½ cups French lentils

1 onion, chopped

1 fennel bulb, peeled and chopped

4 beefsteak tomatoes, seeded and chopped

5 garlic cloves, sliced

5 cups Veggie Broth (page 60)

2 cups water

¼ cup freshly squeezed lemon juice

1 teaspoon dried oregano leaves

1 teaspoon salt

⅛ teaspoon freshly ground black pepper

2 cups fresh green beans, roughly chopped

½ cup crumbled feta cheese

6 tablespoons extra-virgin olive oil

CHIPOTLE-BLACK BEAN STEW

SERVES: 6 • PREP TIME: 25 MINUTES, PLUS OVERNIGHT TO SOAK
COOK TIME: 8 HOURS, 20 MINUTES TO 10 HOURS, 20 MINUTES ON LOW

I find the heat and smokiness of the chipotle chiles to be the star of this thick and rich stew that is also full of vegetables. I like to serve it with some hot cornbread fresh from the oven, or savory scones.

1 pound dried black beans

2 onions, chopped

1½ cups sliced mushrooms

4 garlic cloves, minced

2 red bell peppers, seeded and chopped

2 chipotle chiles in adobo sauce, minced

3 tablespoons adobo sauce

6 cups Veggie Broth (page 60)

1 (14-ounce) can diced tomatoes, undrained

3 tablespoons tomato paste

1 tablespoon chili powder

1 teaspoon salt

⅛ teaspoon freshly ground black pepper

1. Sort the beans, rinse well, and drain. In a 4- or 5-quart slow cooker, cover the beans with cool water. Let stand overnight.

2. In the morning, drain the beans, discarding the soaking liquid. In the slow cooker, stir well to combine the beans, onions, mushrooms, garlic, red bell peppers, chipotle chiles, adobo sauce, Veggie Broth, diced tomatoes, tomato paste, chili powder, salt, and pepper.

3. Cover the slow cooker, and cook on low for 8 to 10 hours, or until the beans are tender.

4. Transfer 1 cup of the soup to a blender or food processor, and purée. Stir the purée back into the soup, and cook on low for another 20 minutes.

5. Stir gently and serve.

JAMBALAYA

SERVES: 6 • PREP TIME: 25 MINUTES • COOK TIME: 8 TO 10 HOURS ON LOW

A good jambalaya can take you on a trip to Cajun country without leaving your home. This delectable vegetarian version—yes, a vegetarian jambalaya— uses tempeh, a soybean-based product that adds a wonderful heartiness to the dish.

1. In a 4- or 5-quart slow cooker, stir well to combine the tempeh, lentils, onion, garlic, red and yellow bell peppers, mushrooms, Veggie Broth, crushed tomatoes, navy beans, tomato paste, paprika, thyme, bay leaf, oregano, salt, black pepper, and cayenne pepper.

2. Cover and cook on low for 8 to 10 hours, or until the vegetables are tender.

3. Remove and discard the thyme stems and the bay leaf.

4. Stir gently and serve.

Perfect Pair

Jambalaya should be served with rice to soak up the sauce. Cook some white or brown rice, and top each serving with a scoop.

2 cups cubed tempeh

1 cup Le Puy lentils, sorted and rinsed

1 onion, chopped

5 garlic cloves, minced

1 red bell pepper, seeded and chopped

1 yellow bell pepper, seeded and chopped

2 cups sliced cremini mushrooms

4 cups Veggie Broth (page 60)

1 (28-ounce) can crushed tomatoes in purée

1 (15-ounce) can navy beans, drained and rinsed

3 tablespoons tomato paste

2 teaspoons ground smoked paprika

2 fresh thyme sprigs

1 dried bay leaf

1 teaspoon dried oregano leaves

1 teaspoon salt

⅛ teaspoon freshly ground black pepper

⅛ teaspoon ground cayenne pepper

CREAMY PUMPKIN SOUP

SERVES: 8 TO 10 • PREP TIME: 25 MINUTES • COOK TIME: 8½ TO 9½ HOURS ON LOW

Pumpkin makes a wonderful, creamy, velvety soup. This recipe is usually made with canned pumpkin, but fresh sugar pumpkins are much better and much more suited to the slow cooker. They are in season from October through December, so it's no wonder this soup is great to serve during holiday gatherings.

3 pounds sugar pumpkins

2 pears, peeled, cored, and cubed

1 onion, finely chopped

5 cups Veggie Broth (page 60)

1 cup pear nectar

2 tablespoons honey

1 teaspoon salt

½ teaspoon ground cinnamon

⅛ teaspoon ground cardamom

⅛ teaspoon ground nutmeg

⅛ teaspoon freshly ground black pepper

1 cup coconut milk

1. Cut the sugar pumpkins in half, and remove the seeds. Cut each half into fourths, and peel each section. Cut the pumpkin flesh into 1-inch cubes.

2. In a 4- or 5-quart slow cooker, stir well to combine the pumpkin cubes, pears, onion, Veggie Broth, pear nectar, honey, salt, cinnamon, cardamom, nutmeg, and pepper.

3. Cover and cook on low for 8 to 9 hours, or until the pumpkin is very tender.

4. Purée the soup using an immersion blender in the slow cooker, or by transferring the soup, in batches, to a food processor or blender (return the puréed soup to the slow cooker).

5. Stir in the coconut milk.

6. Cover and cook on low for 20 to 30 minutes, or until the soup is hot.

7. Stir gently and serve.

Perfect Pair

This soup is wonderful topped with a swirl of sour cream and a sprinkle of pumpkin seeds and cilantro. You can either use the reserved pumpkin seeds from the pumpkins—just toast them in a 350°F oven for 10 to 20 minutes, until lightly golden brown—or find them in the grocery store, where they're often labeled "pepitas."

CHICKPEA *and* SPINACH SOUP

SERVES: 8 • PREP TIME: 25 MINUTES, PLUS OVERNIGHT TO SOAK
COOK TIME: 8 HOURS, 10 MINUTES TO 10 HOURS, 15 MINUTES ON LOW

Chickpeas and spinach are a great combination for a hearty soup. The potatoes, carrots, fennel, and tomatoes—and spinach, of course—add a delightful pop of color to the recipe. I like it even better knowing that it has lots of vitamins A and C.

1. Sort the chickpeas, rinse well, and drain. In a 4- or 5-quart slow cooker or a large bowl, cover the chickpeas with cool water. Let stand overnight.

2. In the morning, drain the chickpeas, discarding the soaking liquid. In the slow cooker, stir well to combine the chickpeas, onion, fennel, carrots, potatoes, garlic, Veggie Broth, tomatoes, bay leaf, marjoram, salt, and pepper.

3. Cover and cook on low for 8 to 10 hours, or until the beans are tender.

4. Remove and discard the bay leaf. Transfer 1 cup of the soup to a blender or food processor, and purée. Stir the purée back into the soup.

5. Rinse the spinach, and tear it into 2-inch pieces. Add the spinach to the slow cooker and stir.

6. Cover and cook on low for another 10 to 15 minutes, or until the spinach is wilted.

7. Stir gently and serve.

1 pound dried chickpeas, sorted and rinsed

2 onions, chopped

1 fennel bulb, peeled and chopped

3 carrots, sliced

3 Yukon Gold potatoes, cubed

4 garlic cloves, minced

5 cups Veggie Broth (page 60)

2 large tomatoes, seeded and chopped

1 dried bay leaf

1 teaspoon dried marjoram leaves

1 teaspoon salt

⅛ teaspoon freshly ground black pepper

6 cups baby spinach leaves

MOROCCAN VEGETABLE STEW

SERVES: 6 TO 8 • PREP TIME: 25 MINUTES • COOK TIME: 8 TO 10 HOURS ON LOW

This recipe is usually cooked in a tagine, a ceramic dish with a funnel-shaped top, for hours. The tagine is kind of an ancient slow cooker. The funneled top catches evaporated liquid and returns it to the food, just like a slow cooker does.

1. In a 4- or 5-quart slow cooker, stir well to combine the onion, carrots, sweet potato, eggplant, tomatoes, garlic, chickpeas, Veggie Broth, ginger root, salt, cumin, turmeric, and pepper.

2. Cover and cook on low for 8 to 10 hours, or until the vegetables are tender.

3. Stir in the olives, mint, and parsley. Ladle the stew into bowls, garnish each serving with a drizzle of olive oil, and serve.

Perfect Pair

Serve this hearty and rich stew with cooked couscous or quinoa. Ladle the stew over a mound of it, or put a large scoop on top.

1 onion, chopped

3 carrots, sliced

1 large sweet potato, peeled and cubed

1 eggplant, peeled and chopped

2 large tomatoes, seeded and chopped

4 garlic cloves, minced

1 (15-ounce) can chickpeas, drained and rinsed

4 cups Veggie Broth (page 60)

2 tablespoons minced ginger root

1 teaspoon salt

1 teaspoon ground cumin

½ teaspoon ground turmeric

⅛ teaspoon freshly ground black pepper

¼ cup finely chopped black olives

¼ cup chopped fresh mint

¼ cup chopped fresh flat-leaf parsley

⅓ cup extra-virgin olive oil

FAJITA CHOWDER

SERVES: 6 • PREP TIME: 25 MINUTES
COOK TIME: 7 HOURS, 15 MINUTES TO 9 HOURS, 20 MINUTES ON LOW

This spicy and colorful chowder is delicious served at a Super Bowl party or after a fall football game. It is very reminiscent of chili, but lighter and healthier. The spicy flavors of fajitas and lots of vegetables, including four kinds of bell peppers, turn this dish into a hearty chowder.

1. In a 4- or 5-quart slow cooker, stir well to combine the onion, red, orange, yellow, and green bell peppers, tomatillos, jalapeños, diced tomatoes with green chiles, garlic, Veggie Broth, chili powder, cumin, salt, and pepper.

2. Cover and cook on low for 7 to 9 hours, or until the vegetables are tender.

3. In a small bowl, mix to combine the cream and cornstarch until smooth with no lumps. Stir the cornstarch mixture into the slow cooker.

4. Cover and cook on low for another 15 to 20 minutes, or until the chowder is slightly thickened.

5. Stir in the cheese and serve.

- 1 red bell pepper, seeded and chopped
- 1 orange bell pepper, seeded and chopped
- 1 yellow bell pepper, seeded and chopped
- 1 green bell pepper, seeded and chopped
- 6 tomatillos, peeled, rinsed, and chopped
- 2 jalapeño peppers, minced
- 1 (14-ounce) can diced tomatoes with green chiles, undrained
- 4 garlic cloves, minced
- 5 cups Veggie Broth (page 60)
- 1 tablespoon chili powder
- 1 teaspoon ground cumin
- 1 teaspoon salt
- 1/8 teaspoon freshly ground black pepper
- 1 cup light cream
- 2 tablespoons cornstarch
- 2 cups shredded Pepper Jack cheese

CHILI & CURRIES

VEGETARIAN CHILI

SERVES: 6 • PREP TIME: 20 MINUTES, PLUS OVERNIGHT TO SOAK
COOK TIME: 7 HOURS, 15 MINUTES TO 9 HOURS, 20 MINUTES ON LOW

Vegetarian chili is one of the best slow cooker recipes around. It's easy to adjust—using your favorite veggies or what you have on hand—to make it your own. The ground beef substitute, made from soy and wheat, is delicious and lends extra heartiness and texture.

1. Sort the kidney and navy beans, rinse well, and drain. In a 4- or 5-quart slow cooker, cover the beans with cool water. Let stand overnight.

2. In the morning, drain the beans, discarding the soaking liquid. In the slow cooker, stir well to combine the beans with the soy crumbles, onions, jalapeños, garlic, diced tomatoes, tomato paste, Veggie Broth, chili powder, cumin, and salt.

3. Cover and cook on low for 7 to 9 hours, or until the beans are tender.

4. Stir in the corn. Cover and cook on high for another 15 to 20 minutes, or until the corn is hot.

5. Stir gently and serve.

- 1 cup dried kidney beans
- 1 cup dried navy beans
- 1 (12-ounce) package frozen soy crumbles
- 2 onions, chopped
- 2 jalapeño peppers, minced
- 5 garlic cloves, minced
- 1 (14-ounce) can diced tomatoes, undrained
- 3 tablespoons tomato paste
- 6 cups Veggie Broth (page 60)
- 1 tablespoon chili powder
- 1 teaspoon ground cumin
- 1 teaspoon salt
- 2 cups frozen corn

Perfect Pair This chili is wonderful topped with some cool guacamole. Just peel and mash 2 or 3 ripe avocados with some freshly squeezed lemon juice and salt. You can add minced jalapeño peppers or chopped fresh tomatoes, but this simple guacamole is perfect, too.

CHICKPEA-COCONUT CURRY

SERVES: 6 • PREP TIME: 20 MINUTES, PLUS OVERNIGHT TO SOAK • COOK TIME: 8 TO 10 HOURS ON LOW

Chickpeas, or garbanzo beans, are one of the best legumes to use for anyone who is leery of going meatless. They are rich and smooth with a nutty and meaty taste. They are delicious in this curry, paired with coconut milk and toasted coconut.

1. Sort the chickpeas, rinse well, and drain. In a 4- or 5-quart slow cooker, cover the chickpeas with cool water. Let stand overnight.

2. In the morning, drain the chickpeas, discarding the soaking water. In the slow cooker, stir well to combine the chickpeas, onion, leek, garlic, carrots, potatoes, Veggie Broth, curry powder, coconut milk, and toasted coconut.

3. Cover and cook on low for 8 to 10 hours, or until the chickpeas are tender.

4. Stir, taste for seasoning (you may want to add more curry powder, since the long cooking time can mute the flavors), and serve.

2½ cups dried chickpeas

1 onion, chopped

1 leek, chopped

4 garlic cloves, minced

4 carrots, sliced

5 Yukon Gold potatoes, peeled and cubed

5 cups Veggie Broth (page 60)

1 to 2 tablespoons curry powder, plus more if desired

1½ cups coconut milk

½ cup toasted coconut shreds (see tip)

Prep It Right

To toast coconut, place it in a dry saucepan over medium heat and toast, stirring frequently, until fragrant and it turns light golden brown, 3 to 5 minutes. Or you can layer the coconut on a baking sheet and bake in a preheated 350°F oven for 4 to 7 minutes. Watch carefully—shredded coconut can go from perfectly toasted to burned very quickly.

CURRIED BEAN TACOS

SERVES: 6 • PREP TIME: 20 MINUTES, PLUS OVERNIGHT TO SOAK • COOK TIME: 8 TO 10 HOURS ON LOW

The nutty flavor of the black beans in these tacos means you won't miss the meat. And curry powder? Absolutely. It is an unusual flavor, adding the taste of India to a Tex-Mex recipe. You can use crisp corn taco shells, warmed in the oven, to hold this spicy filling, or use soft corn or flour tortillas and let everyone build their own.

1. Sort the black beans, rinse well, and drain. In a 4- or 5-quart slow cooker, cover the beans with cool water. Let stand overnight.

2. In the morning, drain the beans, discarding the soaking water. In the slow cooker, stir well to combine the beans, onion, poblano, red bell pepper, tomatillos, jalapeños, garlic, Veggie Broth, curry powder, and ginger.

3. Cover and cook on low for 8 to 10 hours, or until the beans are tender.

4. Mash some of the bean mixture right in the slow cooker using a potato masher, and stir to combine. This helps thicken the mixture a bit.

5. Spoon the bean filling into the crisp taco shells or onto the tortillas, add the desired toppings, and serve.

2 cups dried black beans

1 onion, chopped

1 poblano pepper, seeded and chopped

1 red bell pepper, seeded and chopped

6 tomatillos, peeled, rinsed, and chopped

2 jalapeño peppers, minced

3 garlic cloves, minced

5 cups Veggie Broth (page 60)

1 to 2 tablespoons curry powder

1 teaspoon ground ginger

8 to 10 crisp taco shells or large corn or flour tortillas

Perfect Pair

Toppings for tacos can include shredded lettuce or cabbage, chopped tomatoes, salsa, shredded cheese, chopped green onions, and avocados or guacamole. Prepare the toppings during the last half hour of cooking.

BLACK BEAN-QUINOA CHILI

SERVES: 6 • PREP TIME: 20 MINUTES • COOK TIME: 7 TO 8 HOURS ON LOW

Quinoa adds wonderful flavor and texture to a black bean chili. This grain is nutty and tender and a fantastic protein source. Because this chili has so many tomatoes, which can prevent legumes from softening in the time it takes the quinoa to cook, we're using canned beans.

1. In a 4- or 5-quart slow cooker, stir well to combine the quinoa, onion, garlic, red bell pepper, jalapeños, black beans, diced tomatoes, tomato sauce, tomato paste, Veggie Broth, chili powder, cumin, oregano, salt, black pepper, and cayenne pepper.

2. Cover and cook on low for 7 to 8 hours, or until the quinoa is tender.

3. Stir gently and serve.

Prep It Right

Any recipe that uses dried beans and lots of tomatoes will take at least 8 to 10 hours to cook. The acid in the tomatoes slows down the softening of the beans. Often, as in this recipe, I'll used canned beans instead.

1 cup quinoa, rinsed

1 onion, chopped

4 garlic cloves, minced

1 red bell pepper, seeded and chopped

2 jalapeño peppers, minced

2 (15-ounce) cans black beans, drained and rinsed

1 (14-ounce) can diced tomatoes, undrained

1 (8-ounce) can tomato sauce

¼ cup tomato paste

5 cups Veggie Broth (page 60)

1 tablespoon chili powder

1 teaspoon ground cumin

1 teaspoon dried oregano leaves

1 teaspoon salt

⅛ teaspoon freshly ground black pepper

⅛ teaspoon ground cayenne pepper

BUTTERNUT CHILI

SERVES: 6 • PREP TIME: 25 MINUTES, PLUS OVERNIGHT TO SOAK • COOK TIME: 8 TO 10 HOURS ON LOW

Butternut squash has a nutty sweetness and is delicious paired with black beans in this unique chili. It's perfect for serving before a football game; it will keep everyone warm while cheering the team from the stands.

1. Sort the black beans, rinse well, and drain. In a 4- or 5-quart slow cooker, cover the beans with water. Let stand overnight.

2. In the morning, drain the beans, discarding the cooking liquid. In the slow cooker, stir well to combine the beans, squash, onion, tomatoes, garlic, chipotle chiles, adobo sauce, Veggie Broth, chili powder, oregano, salt, black pepper, and red pepper flakes.

3. Cover and cook on low for 8 to 10 hours, or until the beans and vegetables are tender.

4. Stir gently and serve.

Did You Know? If beans stay tough no matter how long they are cooked, your water may be hard; in other words, it has a lot of minerals. You can add ¼ teaspoon of baking soda to the slow cooker to help neutralize the pH of the liquid so the beans will become tender.

2 cups dried black beans

1 butternut squash, peeled and cubed

1 onion, chopped

3 tomatoes, seeded and chopped

4 garlic cloves, minced

2 chipotle chiles in adobo sauce, minced

2 tablespoons adobo sauce

5 cups Veggie Broth (page 60)

1 tablespoon chili powder

1 teaspoon dried oregano leaves

1 teaspoon salt

¼ teaspoon freshly ground black pepper

⅛ teaspoon crushed red pepper flakes

CURRIED VEGGIES
and WHITE BEANS

SERVES: 6 • PREP TIME: 20 MINUTES, PLUS OVERNIGHT TO SOAK • COOK TIME: 8 TO 10 HOURS ON LOW

I love curry; the fragrance, taste, and color make food look gorgeous and taste wonderful. Vegetables and beans together are delicious when cooked with curry powder and other spices. Tofu adds more protein and texture to this simple recipe.

1. Sort the navy and Great Northern beans, rinse well, and drain. In a 4- or 5-quart slow cooker, and cover the beans with cool water. Let stand overnight.

2. In the morning, drain the beans, discarding the cooking liquid. In the slow cooker, stir well to combine the beans with the onion, sweet potato, carrots, tomatoes, tofu, Veggie Broth, curry powder, turmeric, cinnamon, salt, and pepper.

3. Cover and cook on low for 8 to 10 hours, or until the beans and vegetables are tender.

4. Stir gently and serve.

Perfect Pair

Serve this curry with a teaspoon of mango chutney as a topping, along with toasted pine nuts or crushed peanuts, toasted coconut, and chopped green onions. If you eat dairy, add a dollop of sour cream or Greek yogurt.

1 cup dried navy beans

1 cup dried Great Northern beans

1 onion, chopped

1 large sweet potato, peeled and chopped

3 carrots, sliced

3 tomatoes, seeded and chopped

1 ½ cups cubed firm tofu

6 cups Veggie Broth (page 60)

1 tablespoon curry powder

½ teaspoon ground turmeric

½ teaspoon ground cinnamon

1 teaspoon salt

⅛ teaspoon freshly ground black pepper

RED LENTIL CHILI

SERVES: 6 • PREP TIME: 15 MINUTES • COOK TIME: 7 TO 9 HOURS ON LOW

Lentils make a wonderful chili. Their texture is similar to ground meat, and their nutty flavor is perfect with the tomatoes, vegetables, and beans in this spicy soup. This one is so good, I can't resist eating it for lunch the next day—if I'm lucky enough that there are leftovers.

1. Sort the lentils, rinse well, and drain.

2. In a 4- or 5-quart slow cooker, stir well to combine the lentils, pinto beans, onions, garlic, jalapeño, crushed tomatoes, tomato paste, Veggie Broth, chili powder, cumin, paprika, salt, and pepper.

3. Cover and cook on low for 7 to 9 hours, or until the lentils are tender.

4. Stir gently and serve.

1½ cups red lentils

1 (15-ounce) can pinto beans, drained and rinsed

2 onions, chopped

5 garlic cloves, sliced

1 jalapeño pepper, minced

1 (28-ounce) can crushed tomatoes in purée

3 tablespoons tomato paste

5 cups Veggie Broth (page 60)

1 tablespoon chili powder

1 teaspoon ground cumin

1 teaspoon ground smoked paprika

1 teaspoon salt

⅛ teaspoon freshly ground black pepper

The Next Day

Leftovers are delicious poured over hot baked potatoes that have been split with some butter or olive oil mashed into the flesh. Just heat this chili in the microwave or on the stove top, and spoon over the potato.

ROOT VEGETABLE CURRY

SERVES: 6 • PREP TIME: 25 MINUTES • COOK TIME: 8 TO 10 HOURS ON LOW

Lots of root vegetables make for a hearty curry, so not even dedicated meat eaters will miss the beef. This curry is rich and thick and fragrant. Other root veggies, such as rutabagas, russet potatoes, or carrots, work great in this recipe—you can use whatever you have on hand.

1. In a 4- or 5-quart slow cooker, stir well to combine the onion, squash, sweet potatoes, parsnip, potatoes, garlic, Veggie Broth, curry powder, turmeric, salt, ginger, and pepper.

2. Cover and cook on low for 8 to 10 hours, or until the vegetables are tender.

3. Stir gently, taste for seasoning (you may want to add more curry powder), and serve.

Perfect Pair

This recipe is wonderful served over brown rice. To prepare the rice, combine 1½ cups rice with 3 cups of water or vegetable broth in a saucepan. Bring to a boil, and then reduce the heat to low, cover, and simmer for 30 to 40 minutes, or until the rice is tender.

2 onions, chopped

2 cups cubed butternut squash

2 sweet potatoes, peeled and cubed

1 parsnip, peeled and cubed

4 Yukon Gold potatoes, cubed

4 garlic cloves, sliced

4 cups Veggie Broth (page 60)

1 tablespoon curry powder, plus more if desired

1 teaspoon ground turmeric

1 teaspoon salt

½ teaspoon ground ginger

⅛ teaspoon freshly ground black pepper

WHITE BEAN MUGHLAI CURRY

SERVES: 6 • PREP TIME: 25 MINUTES, PLUS OVERNIGHT TO SOAK
COOK TIME: 8 HOURS, 15 MINUTES TO 10 HOURS, 20 MINUTES ON LOW

Mughlai curry is a mild and rich dish that is finished with cream. Yes, there are a lot of spices in this dish, but they combine and blend to make something special. They are used in addition to curry powder for a complex flavor. The good news is, most of them are probably pantry staples already.

1. Sort the cannellini beans, rinse well, and drain. In a 4- or 5-quart slow cooker, cover the beans with cool water. Let stand overnight.

2. In the morning, drain the beans, discarding the cooking liquid. In the slow cooker, stir well to combine the beans, tofu, onion, cauliflower, poblano, garlic, Veggie Broth, curry powder, cumin, turmeric, saffron, cinnamon, cardamom, nutmeg, and salt.

3. Cover and cook on low for 8 to 10 hours, or until the beans and vegetables are tender.

2 cups dried cannellini beans

1 cup firm tofu, drained and cubed

1 onion, chopped

1½ cups small cauliflower florets

1 poblano pepper, seeded and chopped

4 garlic cloves, minced

6 cups Veggie Broth (page 60)

2 teaspoons curry powder

1 teaspoon ground cumin

1 teaspoon ground turmeric

1 pinch saffron threads

¼ teaspoon ground cinnamon

⅛ teaspoon ground cardamom

⅛ teaspoon ground nutmeg

1 teaspoon salt

1 cup heavy (whipping) cream

2 tablespoons cornstarch

4. In a small bowl, mix well to combine the cream and corn-starch until it is smooth with no lumps. Stir the mixture into the slow cooker.

5. Cover and cook on low for another 15 to 20 minutes, or until the curry is creamy and slightly thickened.

6. Stir gently and serve.

Basmati rice is perfect with this curry. This is a long-grain rice that is fragrant and fluffy. It smells like popcorn while it's cooking! Cook it as you would any white rice, adding a dash of curry powder and cardamom for more flavor.

SPICY RED CHILI

SERVES: 6 • PREP TIME: 25 MINUTES, PLUS OVERNIGHT TO SOAK • COOK TIME: 9 TO 10 HOURS ON LOW

The more beans the better! This chili is rich and suave, with lots of vegetables and seasonings. Adjust the spice level in this recipe to suit your taste. This version has a kick already, but you can certainly add more chiles, red pepper flakes, or hot sauce to spice it up even more.

1. Sort the kidney and pinto beans, rinse well, and drain. In a 4- or 5-quart slow cooker or a large bowl, cover the beans with cool water. Let stand overnight.

2. In the morning, drain the beans, discarding the soaking liquid. In the slow cooker, stir well to combine the beans with the onion, garlic, red bell peppers, tomatoes, tomato paste, jalapeños, Veggie Broth, chili powder, cumin, oregano, salt, black pepper, and red pepper flakes.

3. Cover and cook on low for 9 to 10 hours, or until the beans are tender.

4. Stir gently and serve.

2 cups dried kidney beans

2 cups dried pinto beans

2 onions, chopped

4 garlic cloves, minced

2 red bell peppers, seeded and chopped

4 large tomatoes, seeded and chopped

¼ cup tomato paste

2 jalapeño peppers, minced

8 cups Veggie Broth (page 60)

1 tablespoon chili powder

1 teaspoon ground cumin

1 teaspoon dried oregano leaves

1 teaspoon salt

⅛ teaspoon freshly ground black pepper

⅛ teaspoon crushed red pepper flakes

SPICY WHITE CHILI

SERVES: 6 • PREP TIME: 20 MINUTES, PLUS OVERNIGHT TO SOAK • COOK TIME: 8 TO 10 HOURS ON LOW

This white chili isn't really "white"—although the beans and tofu are. There's lots of amazing green included, from poblanos and jalapeño to tomatillos, green bell pepper, and green salsa. Most important, of course, is that the flavor is out of this world.

1. Sort the navy beans, rinse well, and drain. In a 4- or 5-quart slow cooker, cover the beans with cool water. Let stand overnight.

2. In the morning, drain the beans, discarding the cooking liquid. In the slow cooker, stir well to combine the beans, tofu, onion, poblano, jalapeño, tomatillos, green bell pepper, Veggie Broth, green salsa, chili powder, cumin, salt, and white pepper.

3. Cover and cook on low for 8 to 10 hours, or until the beans and vegetables are tender.

4. Stir gently and serve.

 Prep It Right Tofu is packed in water. Always drain it well before using. Open the package and drain off the liquid. Then layer the tofu between paper towels and press down with your hands. Once most of the liquid has been removed from the tofu, cut it into cubes.

2 cups dried navy beans

1½ cups chopped firm tofu

1 onion, chopped

1 poblano pepper, chopped

1 jalapeño pepper, minced

6 tomatillos, peeled, rinsed, and chopped

1 green bell pepper, seeded and chopped

6 cups Veggie Broth (page 60)

1 cup jarred green salsa

1 tablespoon chili powder

1 teaspoon ground cumin

1 teaspoon salt

⅛ teaspoon freshly ground white pepper

TEMPEH CHILI

SERVES: 6 • PREP TIME: 25 MINUTES • COOK TIME: 7 TO 9 HOURS ON LOW

Tempeh is a wonderful ingredient to use in chili. It has a meat-like texture and rich and nutty taste. When combined with lots of tomatoes, beans, vegetables, and spices, this soy product makes a dish that will satisfy any meat lover.

1. In a 4- or 5-quart slow cooker, stir well to combine the tempeh, onions, red bell pepper, poblano, garlic, chipotle chili, adobo sauce, pinto beans, kidney beans, diced tomatoes, tomato sauce, taco sauce, tomato paste, Veggie Broth, chili powder, salt, and pepper.

2. Cover and cook on low for 7 to 9 hours, or until the chili is slightly thickened and bubbling.

3. Stir gently and serve.

1 (8-ounce) package tempeh, crumbled

2 onions, chopped

1 red bell pepper, seeded and chopped

1 poblano pepper, seeded and chopped

4 garlic cloves, minced

1 chipotle chili in adobo sauce, minced

2 tablespoons adobo sauce

1 (15-ounce) can pinto beans, drained and rinsed

1 (15-ounce) can red kidney beans, drained and rinsed

1 (14-ounce) can diced tomatoes with green chiles, undrained

1 (8-ounce) can tomato sauce

1 (8-ounce) can taco sauce

3 tablespoons tomato paste

2 cups Veggie Broth (page 60)

1 tablespoon chili powder

1 teaspoon salt

⅛ teaspoon freshly ground black pepper

SWEET POTATO CHILI

SERVES: 6 • PREP TIME: 25 MINUTES • COOK TIME: 7 TO 9 HOURS ON LOW

Sweet potatoes are a great ingredient to use in chili. This nutty tasting and sweet root vegetable helps calm the heat of the dish and adds color. They are healthy to boot—full of vitamin A and potassium. Soy crumbles add great texture, but you can omit that product if you'd like and make this chili gluten- and soy-free.

1. In a 4- or 5-quart slow cooker, stir well to combine the sweet potatoes, soy crumbles, onion, garlic, chopped tomatoes, black beans, diced tomatoes, Veggie Broth, chili powder, oregano, and salt.

2. Cover and cook on low for 7 to 9 hours, or until the chili is slightly thickened and bubbling.

3. Stir gently and serve.

 Did You Know? Frozen soy meat substitutes can be purchased in several types and flavors. You can buy "sausage" patties and break them up to add to soups and stews, or buy soy chorizo for a spicier kick.

3 sweet potatoes, peeled and cubed

1 (12-ounce) package frozen soy crumbles

1 onion, chopped

4 garlic cloves, minced

4 large tomatoes, seeded and chopped

2 (15-ounce) cans black beans, drained and rinsed

1 (14-ounce) can diced tomatoes, undrained

4 cups Veggie Broth (page 60)

1 tablespoon chili powder

1 teaspoon dried oregano leaves

1 teaspoon salt

RED BEAN-TOFU CHILI

SERVES: 6 • PREP TIME: 25 MINUTES • COOK TIME: 7 TO 9 HOURS ON LOW

There are two kinds of red beans: kidney beans and, well, red beans. Red beans are smaller and round and can be used as a substitute for kidney beans. If you can't find canned red beans, substitute another can of kidney beans.

1. Drain the tofu, and press it between paper towels until most of the liquid is pressed out. Cut into cubes, and set aside.

2. In a blender or food processor, process the onions, garlic, chipotle chiles, adobo sauce, tomatoes, and tomato paste until the mixture is finely chopped but still a little chunky; don't purée it.

3. In a 4- or 5-quart slow cooker, stir well to combine the onion mixture, tofu, kidney beans, red beans, Veggie Broth, chili powder, marjoram, salt, and pepper.

4. Cover and cook on low for 7 to 9 hours, or until the vegetables are tender.

5. Stir gently and serve over rice, garnished with the green onions.

Perfect Pair

Serve this dish with fluffy medium- or long-grain rice, and add a sprinkle of chopped green onion as garnish.

- 1 (8-ounce) package firm tofu
- 2 onions, chopped
- 4 garlic cloves
- 2 chipotle chiles in adobo sauce
- 2 tablespoons adobo sauce
- 4 large tomatoes, seeded and chopped
- 3 tablespoons tomato paste
- 1 (15-ounce) can kidney beans, drained and rinsed
- 1 (15-ounce) can red beans, drained and rinsed
- 4 cups Veggie Broth (page 60)
- 1 tablespoon chili powder
- 1 teaspoon dried marjoram leaves
- 1 teaspoon salt
- 1/8 teaspoon freshly ground black pepper
- 6 cups cooked rice, brown or white
- 1/3 cup chopped green onions

BUTTERNUT SQUASH CURRY

SERVES: 6 • PREP TIME: 25 MINUTES
COOK TIME: 8 HOURS, 15 MINUTES TO 10 HOURS, 20 MINUTES ON LOW

The flavor profiles of many curries are enhanced with a garnish of fruit chutney. The concentrated sweetness of the fruit is a nice complement with the blend of spices in the dish. Just remember that a little bit of chutney goes a long way; you don't want it to overpower the curry. This butternut squash curry is fabulous served over white or brown rice, topped with mango chutney.

1. In a 4- or 5-quart slow cooker, stir well to combine the squash, onion, garlic, beans, carrots, tomatoes, Veggie Broth, curry powder, turmeric, cumin, ginger, cinnamon, salt, and pepper.

2. Cover and cook on low for 8 to 10 hours, or until the vegetables are tender.

3. Stir in the coconut milk, cover, and cook on low for another 15 to 20 minutes, or until hot.

4. Stir gently and serve.

1 butternut squash, peeled and cubed

2 onions, chopped

4 garlic cloves, minced

1 (15-ounce) can cannellini beans, drained and rinsed

2 carrots, sliced

3 tomatoes, seeded and chopped

2 cups Veggie Broth (page 60)

1 tablespoon curry powder

1 teaspoon ground turmeric

½ teaspoon ground cumin

½ teaspoon ground ginger

½ teaspoon ground cinnamon

1 teaspoon salt

⅛ teaspoon freshly ground black pepper

1 cup coconut milk

Did You Know? Turmeric, which is a bright yellow spice, contains a compound called curcumin, a powerful antioxidant that may help reduce the risk of cancer. The yellow powder can also stain clothing.

CURRIED BARLEY RISOTTO

SERVES: 6 • PREP TIME: 20 MINUTES
COOK TIME: 7 HOURS, 10 MINUTES TO 9 HOURS, 15 MINUTES ON LOW

Hulled barley is used in this "risotto" because it maintains its shape and texture during the long cooking time. You can use pearl barley, too, just be sure to reduce the cooking time to 4 to 5 hours on low or you'll be left with mush—albeit delicious mush.

1. In a 4- or 5-quart slow cooker, stir well to combine the barley, onion, garlic, mushrooms, red and yellow bell peppers, Veggie Broth, curry paste, salt, and pepper.

2. Cover and cook on low for 7 to 9 hours, or until the barley is tender.

3. Stir in the Parmesan cheese and butter, cover, and cook on low for another 10 to 15 minutes, or until the cheese and butter are melted.

4. Stir gently and serve.

2 cups hulled barley

2 onions, chopped

5 garlic cloves, minced

2 cups sliced shiitake mushrooms

1 red bell pepper, seeded and chopped

1 yellow bell pepper, seeded and chopped

5 cups Veggie Broth (page 60)

1 to 2 tablespoons yellow curry paste

1 teaspoon salt

1/8 teaspoon freshly ground black pepper

1 cup grated Parmesan cheese

2 tablespoons butter

Ingredient Tip Curry paste is a combination of spices, such as coriander and turmeric, along with cilantro, lemongrass, ginger, and chiles. It can be purchased at most large grocery stores. The product comes in several colors: green, red, and yellow. Yellow curry paste is usually the mildest. Red curry paste has more heat, and green curries are the hottest, but they also have sweet notes. Be sure to look at the labels, as some brands contain fish.

CURRIED SWEET POTATOES *and* BEANS

SERVES: 6 • PREP TIME: 25 MINUTES • COOK TIME: 8 TO 10 HOURS ON LOW

Even though many people call them "yams," the sweet potatoes available to us are not technically yams. Yams are usually grown in Asia and Africa and are dry and starchy when cooked. They are very rarely found in American grocery stores. Sweet potatoes can be white, yellow, or orange and become moist and soft—and sweet—when cooked.

1. In a 4- or 5-quart slow cooker, stir well to combine the sweet potatoes, onion, garlic, beans, tomatoes, curry paste, Veggie Broth, curry powder, turmeric, ginger, honey, salt, and pepper.

2. Cover and cook on low for 8 to 10 hours, or until the sweet potatoes are tender.

3. Stir gently and serve.

4 sweet potatoes, peeled and cubed

2 onions, chopped

5 garlic cloves, sliced

2 (15-ounce) cans navy beans, drained and rinsed

1 (14-ounce) can diced tomatoes, undrained

2 tablespoons yellow or red curry paste

2 cups Veggie Broth (page 60)

2 teaspoons curry powder

1 teaspoon ground turmeric

1 teaspoon ground ginger

1 tablespoon honey

1 teaspoon salt

⅛ teaspoon freshly ground black pepper

The Next Day This dish can be reincarnated as a soup the next day. Just purée everything in a blender or food processor, adding more Veggie Broth or some coconut milk as needed for the right consistency.

TOFU-VEGGIE CURRY

SERVES: 6 • PREP TIME: 25 MINUTES • COOK TIME: 7 TO 9 HOURS ON LOW

Tofu absorbs the flavors of whatever it's cooked with, making it a kitchen chameleon. Every bite of this rich curry dish will have the flavors of cardamom, cumin, coriander, and ginger. You can use just about any vegetable you'd like in this delicious dish.

1. Drain the tofu, and place the blocks between paper towels. Press down on the tofu to remove most of the liquid. Cut into 1-inch cubes.

2. In a 4- or 5-quart slow cooker, stir well to combine the tofu, onion, garlic, ginger root, sweet potato, carrots, mushrooms, beans, diced tomatoes, tomato paste, Veggie Broth, curry paste, curry powder, salt, and pepper.

3. Cover and cook on low for 7 to 9 hours, or until the vegetables are tender.

4. Stir gently and serve.

2 (8-ounce) packages firm tofu

1 onion, chopped

3 garlic cloves, minced

1 tablespoon minced fresh ginger root

1 sweet potato, peeled and cubed

2 carrots, sliced

2 cups sliced cremini mushrooms

1 (15-ounce) can cannellini beans, drained and rinsed

1 (14-ounce) can diced tomatoes, undrained

3 tablespoons tomato paste

3 cups Veggie Broth (page 60)

1 to 2 tablespoons red curry paste

2 teaspoons curry powder

1 teaspoon salt

⅛ teaspoon freshly ground black pepper

SUMMER VEGETABLE CHILI

SERVES: 6 • PREP TIME: 25 MINUTES
COOK TIME: 5 HOURS, 15 MINUTES TO 7 HOURS, 20 MINUTES ON LOW

Summer vegetables can make a wonderful chili. They provide a note of freshness and color to this healthy and flavorful recipe. Quinoa is added to this chili recipe for more protein and a great texture.

1. Rinse the quinoa well and drain.

2. In a 4- or 5-quart slow cooker, stir well to combine the quinoa, onion, red bell pepper, poblano, yellow squash, zucchini, garlic, chickpeas, Veggie Broth, diced tomatoes, chili powder, cumin, paprika, salt, black pepper, and red pepper flakes.

3. Cover and cook on low for 5 to 7 hours, or until the vegetables are tender.

4. Stir in the kale, cover, and cook on low for another 15 to 20 minutes, or until the kale is just tender.

5. Stir gently and serve.

1 cup quinoa

2 onions, chopped

1 red bell pepper, seeded and chopped

1 poblano pepper, seeded and chopped

2 yellow summer squash, chopped

1 zucchini, chopped

4 garlic cloves, minced

2 (15-ounce) cans chickpeas, drained and rinsed

4 cups Veggie Broth (page 60)

1 (14-ounce) can diced tomatoes with chiles, undrained

1 tablespoon chili powder

1 teaspoon ground cumin

1 teaspoon ground smoked paprika

1 teaspoon salt

⅛ teaspoon freshly ground black pepper

⅛ teaspoon crushed red pepper flakes

4 cups torn kale

SWEET POTATO-LENTIL CURRY

SERVES: 6 • PREP TIME: 25 MINUTES
COOK TIME: 7 HOURS, 15 MINUTES TO 9 HOURS, 20 MINUTES ON LOW

Sweet potatoes and lentils pair very well together in this spicy dish. You can use any color of curry paste you'd like in this recipe, and add other vegetables according to your tastes; try sliced carrots or some chopped red or yellow bell peppers. I prefer yellow curry paste because it's milder, with a creamy consistency.

1. In a 4- or 5-quart slow cooker, stir well to combine the sweet potato, lentils, onion, leek, garlic, curry paste, Veggie Broth, turmeric, ginger, cardamom, salt, and pepper.

2. Cover and cook on low for 7 to 9 hours, or until the potatoes are tender and the lentils are soft.

3. In a small bowl, mix well to combine the coconut milk and cornstarch until smooth with no lumps. Stir the mixture into the slow cooker.

4. Cover and cook on low for another 15 to 20 minutes, or until the liquid is thickened.

5. Stir gently and serve.

3 sweet potatoes, peeled and cubed

1 cup red lentils, sorted and rinsed

1 onion, chopped

1 leek, chopped

3 garlic cloves, minced

1 tablespoon red or yellow curry paste

3 cups Veggie Broth (page 60)

1 teaspoon ground turmeric

½ teaspoon ground ginger

⅛ teaspoon ground cardamom

1 teaspoon salt

⅛ teaspoon freshly ground black pepper

1 cup coconut milk

1 tablespoon cornstarch

Perfect Pair This creamy and rich recipe is even better when served with a crisp green salad for a texture, temperature, and flavor contrast. Toss the salad greens with chopped avocado, grape tomatoes, and a light vinaigrette.

MOLE CHILI

SERVES: 6 • PREP TIME: 25 MINUTES • COOK TIME: 8 TO 10 HOURS ON LOW

Mole is a dark, deep, and rich sauce from the Oaxaca region of Mexico. Unsweetened dark chocolate or cocoa is added to create a unique flavor profile. But it doesn't taste like chocolate—instead it gives the sauce a smoky and rich taste.

1. In a 4- or 5-quart slow cooker, stir well to combine the onion, garlic, chipotle chiles, adobo sauce, chopped tomatoes, kidney and pinto beans, diced tomatoes, Veggie Broth, salsa, chocolate, chili powder, cumin, paprika, salt, and pepper.

2. Cover and cook on low for 8 to 10 hours, or until the chili is thickened and simmering.

3. Stir gently and serve.

The Next Day Leftovers of this spicy and sophisticated chili can be served over pasta. Use linguine, fettuccine, or spaghetti noodles.

2 onions, chopped

4 garlic cloves, minced

2 chipotle chiles in adobo sauce, minced

2 tablespoons adobo sauce

4 large tomatoes, seeded and chopped

2 (15-ounce) cans kidney beans, drained and rinsed

1 (15-ounce) can pinto beans, drained and rinsed

1 (14-ounce) can diced tomatoes with chiles, undrained

3 cups Veggie Broth (page 60)

1 cup salsa

1 (1-ounce) square unsweetened baking chocolate, chopped

1 tablespoon chili powder

1 teaspoon ground cumin

1 teaspoon ground smoked paprika

1 teaspoon salt

⅛ teaspoon freshly ground black pepper

MOROCCAN CHILI

SERVES: 6 • PREP TIME: 25 MINUTES, PLUS 40 MINUTES TO STAND • COOK TIME: 8 TO 10 HOURS ON LOW

Moroccan flavors are a fusion of Middle Eastern, North African, and Mediterranean cuisines. Common ingredients used in Moroccan cooking include couscous, eggplant, olive oil, cinnamon, ginger, saffron, cloves, anise, oregano, and bay leaves. Harissa, a hot and spicy chili paste, adds a great kick to this recipe.

1. On a wire rack, sprinkle the eggplant with ½ teaspoon of salt. Let stand for 30 minutes, and then rinse the slices to remove excess salt. Pat the eggplant dry with paper towels, and chop the slices into pieces.

2. In a 4- or 5-quart slow cooker, stir well to combine the eggplant, the remaining ½ teaspoon of salt, and the onion, garlic, jalapeño, mushrooms, chickpeas, tomatoes, Veggie Broth, harissa, chili powder, cinnamon, ginger, saffron, cloves, oregano, bay leaves, red pepper flakes, and black pepper.

3. Cover and cook on low for 8 to 10 hours, or until the vegetables are tender.

4. Remove and discard the bay leaf. Stir in the couscous, cover, and let stand for 10 minutes, or until the couscous is tender.

5. Stir gently and serve.

Eggplant can release a lot of water when cooked in the slow cooker, so it's salted before cooking to remove excess moisture. Salting also improves the texture of this vegetable and helps it better hold its form.

1 medium eggplant, sliced

1 teaspoon salt, divided

2 onions, chopped

5 garlic cloves, minced

2 jalapeño peppers, minced

1 ½ cups sliced cremini mushrooms

1 (15-ounce) can chickpeas, drained and rinsed

1 (14-ounce) can diced tomatoes with green chiles, undrained

2 cups Veggie Broth (page 60)

1 tablespoon harissa

1 tablespoon chili powder

½ teaspoon ground cinnamon

½ teaspoon ground ginger

Pinch saffron threads

⅛ teaspoon ground cloves

1 teaspoon dried oregano leaves

2 dried bay leaves

¼ teaspoon crushed red pepper flakes

⅛ teaspoon freshly ground black pepper

½ cup couscous

INDIAN CAULIFLOWER

SERVES: 6 • PREP TIME: 25 MINUTES • COOK TIME: 8 TO 9 HOURS ON LOW

Some of the sumptuous flavors used in Indian cuisine include coriander, cumin, cinnamon, cardamom, and cayenne pepper. These flavorful spices turn a simple stew into a feast.

1. Remove the leaves from the cauliflower and discard; rinse the cauliflower. Cut the florets off the cauliflower, and chop the stems into 1-inch pieces.

2. In a 4- or 5-quart slow cooker, stir well to combine the stems and florets with the onion, garlic, potatoes, Veggie Broth, chickpeas, tomatoes, rice, mustard, honey, salt, curry powder, cumin, cinnamon, cardamom, nutmeg, black pepper, and cayenne pepper.

3. Cover and cook on low for 8 to 9 hours, or until the vegetables are tender.

4. Stir gently and serve.

1 large head cauliflower

2 onions, chopped

5 garlic cloves, minced

5 Yukon Gold potatoes, peeled and cubed

5 cups Veggie Broth (page 60)

1 (15-ounce) can chickpeas, drained and rinsed

4 large tomatoes, seeded and chopped

1 cup long-grain brown rice

2 tablespoons Dijon mustard

2 tablespoons honey

1 teaspoon salt

2 teaspoons curry powder

1 teaspoon ground cumin

½ teaspoon ground cinnamon

⅛ teaspoon ground cardamom

⅛ teaspoon ground nutmeg

¼ teaspoon freshly ground black pepper

⅛ teaspoon ground cayenne pepper

CASSEROLES & LAYERED DISHES

VEGGIE MAC *and* CHEESE

SERVES: 6 • PREP TIME: 25 MINUTES • COOK TIME: 6 TO 8 HOURS ON LOW

Pasta is tricky to cook in the slow cooker. More than 2 hours, and white flour pasta becomes mushy and may completely dissolve. Whole-wheat pasta stands up far better—so helpful since it's healthier, too—and I like to use it in this veggie mac and cheese. I prefer a sturdier pasta than elbow macaroni as well.

1. In a 4- or 5-quart slow cooker, stir well to combine the pasta, onion, garlic, carrots, and mushrooms.

2. In a large bowl, whisk the water, milk, eggs, and egg whites until combined. Pour the mixture into the slow cooker, and stir.

3. Add the Cheddar, Monterey Jack, and Parmesan cheeses, salt, and pepper, and stir again.

4. Cover and cook on low for 6 to 8 hours, or until the pasta is tender, stirring occasionally if you are at home while the food is cooking.

5. Stir gently and serve.

1 (16-ounce) box whole-wheat penne or mostaccioli pasta

1 onion, chopped

2 garlic cloves, minced

3 carrots, sliced

2 cups sliced cremini mushrooms

3 cups water

3 cups whole milk

3 eggs

2 egg whites

4 cups shredded Cheddar cheese

2 cups shredded Monterey Jack cheese

1 cup grated Parmesan cheese

1 teaspoon salt

⅛ teaspoon freshly ground black pepper

Perfect Pair

A seasonal fruit salad is a great accompaniment to this mild, creamy recipe. In winter, choose apples, oranges, and grapes. In the summer, strawberries, blueberries, and raspberries are delicious.

CHEESY VEGGIE SPAGHETTI

SERVES: 6 • PREP TIME: 20 MINUTES
COOK TIME: 8 HOURS, 15 MINUTES TO 10 HOURS, 30 MINUTES ON LOW

Spaghetti cooks very well in the slow cooker when it's added during the last 20 to 30 minutes of cooking time. You just have to make sure that the pasta is completely submerged in the sauce or you'll end up with parts of noodles perfectly cooked while other parts are not.

1. In a 4- or 5-quart slow cooker, stir well to combine the onion, garlic, mushrooms, red bell pepper, crushed tomatoes, tomato paste, Veggie Broth, basil, oregano, thyme, salt, and pepper.

2. Cover and cook on low for 8 to 10 hours, or until the vegetables are tender.

3. Stir in the pasta, cover, and cook on low for another 15 to 30 minutes, or until the pasta is tender.

4. Stir in the Parmesan cheese and serve.

1 onion, chopped

2 garlic cloves, minced

2 cups sliced mushrooms

1 red bell pepper, seeded and chopped

1 (28-ounce) can crushed tomatoes

3 tablespoons tomato paste

3 cups Veggie Broth (page 60)

1 teaspoon dried basil leaves

1 teaspoon dried oregano leaves

1 teaspoon dried thyme leaves

1 teaspoon salt

1/8 teaspoon freshly ground black pepper

1 (12-ounce) package spaghetti, broken in half

1 cup grated Parmesan cheese

SPINACH *and* LENTIL CASSEROLE

SERVES: 6 • PREP TIME: 20 MINUTES • COOK TIME: 7 HOURS 10 MINUTES TO 9 HOURS, 10 MINUTES ON LOW

Lentils and spinach are a delicious, classic combination. The sweetness of the lentils and their texture plays off well against the slightly bitter spinach. The mushrooms and other vegetables add a richness and round out this casserole.

2 cups Le Puy (French) lentils

1 onion, chopped

1 leek, chopped

3 celery stalks, sliced

1 cup sliced mushrooms

1 red bell pepper, seeded and chopped

3 garlic cloves, minced

4 cups Veggie Broth (page 60)

1 teaspoon dried marjoram leaves

1 teaspoon salt

⅛ teaspoon freshly ground black pepper

3 cups baby spinach leaves

½ cup grated Parmesan cheese

1. Sort the lentils, rinse well, and drain.

2. In a 4- or 5-quart slow cooker, stir well to combine the lentils, onion, leek, celery, mushrooms, red bell pepper, garlic, Veggie Broth, marjoram, salt, and pepper.

3. Cover and cook on low for 7 to 9 hours, or until the lentils and vegetables are tender.

4. Stir in the spinach, cover, and cook on low for another 10 minutes, or until the spinach is wilted.

5. Stir in the Parmesan cheese and serve.

Prep It Right Spinach can be very gritty, since it is grown in loose, sandy soil. Make sure that you rinse it well. Put the spinach in a large bowl of cool water, and agitate gently with your hands. The sand will fall to the bottom of the bowl. Lift out the leaves, rinse them under running water, and dry on paper towels.

SWEET and SOUR LENTILS

SERVES: 6 • PREP TIME: 25 MINUTES • COOK TIME: 6 TO 8 HOURS ON LOW

The ingredients that make this recipe "sour" are also the ingredients that help the lentils keep their shape and texture as they cook. Tamarind paste is made from a sour fruit that grows in the tropics. It's common in Thai recipes and adds a great flavor to many dishes, this one included.

1. Sort the lentils, rinse well, and drain.

2. In a 4- or 5-quart slow cooker, stir well to combine the lentils, onion, garlic, ginger root, sweet potatoes, carrots, Veggie Broth, apple juice, pineapple, honey, lemon juice, tamarind paste, salt, and pepper.

3. Cover and cook on low for 6 to 8 hours, or until the lentils and vegetables are tender.

4. Stir gently and serve.

Perfect Pair Serve this recipe with white or brown rice or quinoa. Garnish the top with some freshly cut, cubed pineapple and green onions for a nice taste, texture, and temperature contrast.

3 cups green lentils

2 onions, chopped

3 garlic cloves, minced

1 tablespoon minced fresh ginger root

2 sweet potatoes, peeled and cubed

3 carrots, sliced

4 cups Veggie Broth (page 60)

1 cup apple juice

1 (8-ounce) can crushed pineapple, undrained

⅓ cup honey

¼ cup freshly squeezed lemon juice

2 tablespoons tamarind paste

1 teaspoon salt

⅛ teaspoon freshly ground black pepper

HAWAIIAN SWEET POTATOES *and* BEANS

SERVES: 6 • PREP TIME: 25 MINUTES, PLUS OVERNIGHT TO SOAK
COOK TIME: 8 HOURS, 20 MINUTES TO 10 HOURS, 30 MINUTES

It may seem strange, but pineapple, coconut milk, navy beans, and sweet potatoes together make a luscious and unusual recipe. The sweet and sour flavors are the perfect complement to the sweet potatoes. Walnuts and toasted coconut add a nutty flavor and nice crunchy texture.

1. Sort the beans, rinse well, and drain. In a 4- or 5-quart slow cooker, cover the beans with cool water. Let stand overnight.

2. In the morning, drain the beans, discarding the soaking liquid. In the slow cooker, stir well to combine the beans, sweet potatoes, onions, red bell pepper, garlic, Veggie Broth, coconut milk, honey, salt, and pepper.

3. Cover and cook on low for 8 to 10 hours, or until the beans are tender.

4. Stir in the pineapple, ketchup, and walnuts. Cover and cook on low for another 20 to 30 minutes, or until the mixture is hot.

5. Stir gently, ladle into bowls, and garnish each with the toasted coconut.

1 cup dried navy beans

3 sweet potatoes, peeled and cubed

2 onions, chopped

2 red bell peppers, seeded and chopped

4 garlic cloves, minced

3 cups Veggie Broth (page 60)

1 cup coconut milk

¼ cup honey

1 teaspoon salt

⅛ teaspoon freshly ground black pepper

1 (8-ounce) can crushed pineapple, undrained

½ cup ketchup

½ cup coarsely chopped walnuts

½ cup toasted coconut, for garnish

CORN and BLACK BEAN ENCHILADAS

SERVES: 6 • PREP TIME: 20 MINUTES • COOK TIME: 7 TO 8 HOURS ON LOW

This recipe isn't technically an enchilada, because the tortillas are layered with the corn and bean mixture rather than being rolled up. But everything about the taste and texture screams enchilada goodness. This hearty recipe is comforting and delicious and a definite crowd pleaser.

1. In a large microwave-safe bowl, mix to combine the olive oil, onions, and garlic. Microwave on high for 2 to 3 minutes, stirring once, until the vegetables are tender.

2. Add the beans, soy crumbles, corn, jalapeños, chili powder, cumin, salsa, tomato sauce, and olives to the bowl, and stir to combine.

3. In the bottom of a 4- or 5-quart slow cooker, put ½ cup of this sauce. Place 4 corn tortillas on top of the sauce in the slow cooker. Top the tortillas with one-third of the remaining sauce mixture, followed by one-third each of the Pepper Jack and Cheddar cheeses. Repeat these layers, ending with the cheeses.

4. Cover and cook on low for 7 to 8 hours, or until the mixture is bubbling and the tortillas are tender.

5. Carefully cut and scoop to serve.

- 1 tablespoon olive oil
- 2 onions, chopped
- 4 garlic cloves, minced
- 1 (15-ounce) can black beans, drained and rinsed
- 1 (12-ounce) package frozen soy crumbles
- 2 cups frozen corn
- 2 jalapeño peppers, minced
- 1 tablespoon chili powder
- 1 teaspoon ground cumin
- 1 (16-ounce) jar salsa
- 1 (8-ounce) can tomato sauce
- ⅓ cup chopped pitted black olives
- 12 (6-inch) corn tortillas
- 2 cups shredded Pepper Jack cheese, divided
- 1 cup shredded Cheddar cheese, divided

Perfect Pair Garnish this hearty recipe with some guacamole, more shredded cheese, and salsa. The combination of hot casserole and cool toppings is delicious. A sprinkle of green onions on top, and dinner is served.

CHEESY VEGETARIAN LASAGNA

SERVES: 6 • PREP TIME: 15 MINUTES • COOK TIME: 6 TO 8 HOURS ON LOW

Lasagna is one of my all-time favorite comfort foods. This version is loaded with vegetables and cheese. I like using whole-wheat lasagna noodles. Not only are they healthier than noodles made from white flour, they take longer to cook in the slow cooker, too.

1. In a large microwave-safe bowl, mix to combine the olive oil, onion, and garlic. Microwave on high for 2 to 3 minutes, or until the vegetables are tender, stirring once.

2. Add the red and green bell peppers, mushrooms, pasta sauce, diced tomatoes, tomato sauce, Veggie Broth, oregano, basil, salt, and black pepper to the bowl, and stir well.

3. In the bottom of a 4- or 5-quart slow cooker, put ½ cup of this mixture. Top with three of the lasagna noodles, broken if necessary so they fit. Top with one-third of the provolone cheese followed by one-third of the remaining sauce mixture. Repeat the layers of sauce, noodles, and cheese, ending with the provolone cheese.

1 tablespoon olive oil

1 onion, chopped

4 garlic cloves, minced

1 red bell pepper, seeded and chopped

1 green bell pepper, seeded and chopped

2 cups sliced mushrooms

3 cups Fresh Tomato-Basil Sauce (page 68), Caramelized Onion-Tomato Sauce (page 72), or 1 (24-ounce) jar pasta sauce

1 (14-ounce) can diced tomatoes, undrained

1 (8-ounce) can tomato sauce

1 cup Veggie Broth (page 60)

1 teaspoon dried oregano leaves

1 teaspoon dried basil leaves

½ teaspoon salt

⅛ teaspoon freshly ground black pepper

9 whole-wheat uncooked lasagna noodles, divided

3 cups shredded provolone cheese, divided

½ cup grated Parmesan cheese

4. Sprinkle the Parmesan cheese over the top.

5. Cover and cook on low for 6 to 8 hours, or until the noodles are tender. Stick a fork into the lasagna noodles to test that they are done.

6. Turn off the slow cooker and let stand, covered, for 45 to 55 minutes so the liquid can be absorbed.

7. Carefully cut and scoop to serve.

Onions can be difficult to cook through in the slow cooker in layered casseroles, but you can omit the microwave cooking step if you prefer and add them raw to the slow cooker.

WILD MUSHROOM STROGANOFF

SERVES: 6 • PREP TIME: 15 MINUTES, PLUS 1 HOUR TO SOAK
COOK TIME: 8 HOURS, 15 MINUTES TO 10 HOURS, 25 MINUTES ON LOW

Wild mushrooms add a smoky, earthy, and exotic flavor to stroganoff, which in itself is simply a mixture of vegetables and usually meat—here, though, we just use loads of veggies. The sauce that results is deep and rich, and sour cream finishes the dish perfectly.

1. In a large bowl, cover the dried porcini, chanterelle, and morel mushrooms with the warm water. Cover and let stand for 1 hour.

2. Drain the mushrooms, reserving the soaking liquid. Strain the soaking liquid through cheesecloth to remove any grit. Cut off and discard the mushroom stems if they are tough or woody.

3. In a 4- or 5-quart slow cooker, stir well to combine the soaked mushrooms, soaking liquid, onions, cremini and button mushrooms, garlic, tomatoes, marjoram, salt, and pepper.

1 ounce dried porcini mushrooms

1 ounce dried chanterelle mushrooms

1 ounce dried morel mushrooms

2 cups warm water

2 onions, chopped

2 cups sliced cremini mushrooms

2 cups sliced button mushrooms

3 garlic cloves, minced

3 large tomatoes, seeded and chopped

1 teaspoon dried marjoram leaves

1 teaspoon salt

⅛ teaspoon freshly ground black pepper

1½ cups sour cream

¼ cup cornstarch

3 tablespoons Dijon mustard

4. Cover and cook on low for 8 to 10 hours, or until the mushrooms are tender.

5. In a medium bowl, mix well to combine the sour cream, cornstarch, and mustard until smooth with no lumps. Add 1 cup of the hot liquid from the slow cooker to the bowl, and whisk until combined with the sour cream.

6. Stir the sour cream mixture into the slow cooker, cover, and cook on low for another 15 to 25 minutes, or until the liquid is thickened.

7. Stir gently and serve.

This recipe should be served over hot cooked egg noodles. If you are avoiding gluten, try one of the varieties of gluten-free noodles on the market. Cook them according to package directions.

LENTIL BEAN TACO BAKE

SERVES: 6 • PREP TIME: 15 MINUTES • COOK TIME: 7 TO 9 HOURS ON LOW

Lentils don't take as long to cook as dried beans, so canned beans are used in this hearty and spicy recipe, and the lentils are able to maintain their shape and texture. I love the combination of these two legumes with vegetables, peppers, and lots of seasonings.

1. Sort the lentils, rinse well, and drain.

2. In a 4- or 5-quart slow cooker, stir well to combine the lentils, onion, garlic, jalapeño, poblano, chipotle chile, adobo sauce, tomato sauce, salsa, Veggie Broth, beans, chili powder, cumin, oregano, salt, and pepper.

3. Cover and cook on low for 7 to 9 hours, or until the lentils and vegetables are tender.

4. Stir gently and serve.

The Next Day

You can use leftovers of this recipe to make tacos the next day. Just heat up the lentil mixture and serve in crisp heated taco shells with shredded cheese, lettuce, chopped avocados, and chopped tomatoes.

1 cup Le Puy lentils

1 onion, chopped

2 garlic cloves, minced

1 jalapeño pepper, minced

1 poblano pepper, seeded and chopped

1 chipotle chile in adobo sauce, minced

1 tablespoon adobo sauce

1 (8-ounce) can tomato sauce

1 cup salsa

2 cups Veggie Broth (page 60)

2 (14-ounce) cans small red beans or kidney beans, drained and rinsed

1 tablespoon chili powder

1 teaspoon ground cumin

1 teaspoon dried oregano leaves

1 teaspoon salt

⅛ teaspoon freshly ground black pepper

CHEESY BROWN RICE CASSEROLE

SERVES: 6 • PREP TIME: 25 MINUTES • COOK TIME: 6 TO 7 HOURS ON LOW

Rice comes in three lengths: short, medium, and long. Short-grain rice is used to make sticky rice for many Asian recipes and for risotto since it releases starch as it cooks. Medium-grain rice is also fairly sticky when cooked and is used in recipes like paella. Long-grain rice is best for the slow cooker. It results in a fluffier finished dish as the grains stay better separated when cooked.

1. In a 4- or 5-quart slow cooker, stir well to combine the onion, leek, garlic, mushrooms, carrots, tomatoes, rice, lentils, Veggie Broth, bay leaf, salt, thyme, and pepper.

2. Cover and cook on low for 6 to 7 hours, or until the rice, lentils, and vegetables are tender.

3. Stir in the cheese, and let stand for 10 minutes.

4. Stir gently and serve.

1 onion, chopped

1 leek, chopped

3 garlic cloves, minced

2 cups sliced mushrooms

3 carrots, sliced

3 tomatoes, seeded and chopped

2 cups long-grain brown rice

1 cup green lentils

5 cups Veggie Broth (page 60)

1 dried bay leaf

1 teaspoon salt

1 teaspoon dried thyme leaves

⅛ teaspoon freshly ground black pepper

1½ cups shredded Havarti or Swiss cheese

BARLEY-BLACK BEAN LAYERED BURRITOS

SERVES: 6 • PREP TIME: 15 MINUTES • COOK TIME: 7 TO 9 HOURS ON LOW

Serve this burrito filling with tortillas and bowls of sour cream, salsas, guacamole, and other favorite fillings, and let everyone construct their own. No two burritos will be alike. It's an instant party—and it's great for kids to be involved in making their own food.

1. In a 4- or 5-quart slow cooker, stir well to combine the barley, onion, garlic, tomatoes, jalapeños, black beans, Veggie Broth, chipotle chile, adobo sauce, chili powder, cumin, lemon juice, salt, black pepper, and cayenne pepper.

2. Cover and cook on low for 7 to 9 hours, or until the barley is tender.

3. Stir gently, and let everyone build their own burrito using the tortillas, cheese, lettuce, salsa, and grape tomatoes.

The Next Day These leftovers make great enchiladas. Roll up the mixture, along with cheese and salsa, in flour tortillas and place in a casserole dish. Pour bottled enchilada sauce over all, sprinkle with more cheese, and bake at 375°F until hot. Hatch Enchilada Sauce, available in both red and green varieties, is made with chiles grown in New Mexico.

1 cup hulled barley

2 onions, chopped

4 garlic cloves, minced

3 tomatoes, seeded and chopped

2 jalapeño peppers, minced

2 (15-ounce) cans black beans, drained and rinsed

2 cups Veggie Broth (page 60)

1 chipotle chile in adobo sauce, minced

2 tablespoons adobo sauce

1 tablespoon chili powder

1 teaspoon ground cumin

2 tablespoons freshly squeezed lemon juice

1 teaspoon salt

⅛ teaspoon freshly ground black pepper

⅛ teaspoon ground cayenne pepper

12 corn or flour tortillas

2 cups shredded cheese

2 cups shredded lettuce

1 cup salsa

1 cup halved grape tomatoes

QUINOA TEX-MEX CASSEROLE

SERVES: 6 • PREP TIME: 25 MINUTES • COOK TIME: 7 TO 9 HOURS ON LOW

I consider Tex-Mex recipes to be milder than traditional Mexican recipes. The combination of pinto beans and corn is classic Mexican. Quinoa is native to the Andes in South America, and the chili powder and vegetables add a Texan twist.

1. In a 4- or 5-quart slow cooker, stir well to combine the quinoa, onions, garlic, red and yellow bell peppers, beans, chopped tomatoes, corn, tomato sauce, salsa, Veggie Broth, chili powder, ancho chili powder, marjoram, oregano, salt, black pepper, and red pepper flakes.

2. Cover and cook on low for 7 to 9 hours, or until the quinoa and vegetables are tender.

3. Stir gently and serve.

Perfect Pair These spicy Tex-Mex recipes are delicious served with lots of toppings. Offer sour cream, Greek yogurt, guacamole, chopped tomatoes, salsa, shredded cheese, lettuce, or any other options you can think of.

2 cups quinoa, well rinsed

2 onions, chopped

4 garlic cloves, minced

1 red bell pepper, seeded and chopped

1 yellow bell pepper, seeded and chopped

2 (15-ounce) cans pinto beans, drained and rinsed

4 large tomatoes, seeded and chopped

1½ cups frozen corn

1 (8-ounce) can tomato sauce

1 cup salsa

2 cups Veggie Broth (page 60)

2 teaspoons chili powder

2 teaspoons ancho chili powder

1 teaspoon dried marjoram leaves

1 teaspoon dried oregano leaves

1 teaspoon salt

⅛ teaspoon freshly ground black pepper

⅛ teaspoon crushed red pepper flakes

ROOT VEGETABLE-TEMPEH STROGANOFF

SERVES: 6 TO 8 • PREP TIME: 25 MINUTES
COOK TIME: 7 HOURS, 10 MINUTES TO 9 HOURS, 15 MINUTES ON LOW

Tempeh and root vegetables make a flavorful stroganoff with a wonderful texture. To make it vegan, simply swap the sour cream with a dairy-free version in this recipe.

1. In a 4- or 5-quart slow cooker, stir well to combine the tempeh, onion, garlic, sweet potatoes, parsnip, carrots, mushrooms, tomatoes, Veggie Broth, soy sauce, smoked paprika, marjoram, salt, and pepper.

2. Cover and cook on low for 7 to 9 hours, or until the vegetables are tender.

3. In a medium bowl, mix to combine the sour cream and cornstarch. Stir in 1 cup hot liquid from the slow cooker, and whisk.

4. Stir the sour cream mixture into the slow cooker, cover, and cook on low for 10 to 15 minutes, or until the sauce has thickened.

5. Stir gently and serve.

2 (8-ounce) packages tempeh, crumbled

1 onion, chopped

3 garlic cloves, minced

3 large sweet potatoes, peeled and cubed

1 large parsnip, peeled and cubed

3 carrots, sliced

2 cups sliced cremini mushrooms

1 (14-ounce) can diced tomatoes, undrained

3 cups Veggie Broth (page 60)

1 tablespoon soy sauce

1 teaspoon ground smoked paprika

1 teaspoon dried marjoram leaves

1 teaspoon salt

½ teaspoon freshly ground black pepper

1 cup sour cream

3 tablespoons cornstarch

CASSOULET

SERVES: 6 • PREP TIME: 15 MINUTES, PLUS OVERNIGHT, PLUS 30 MINUTES TO SOAK
COOK TIME: 8 TO 10 HOURS ON LOW, PLUS 5 MINUTES ON THE STOVE TOP

Cassoulet is a French dish traditionally made with lots of meat and sausages. But it can be made vegetarian and hearty by using beans, mushrooms, caramelized onions, and lots of vegetables. This dish is topped with toasted bread crumbs but these can be eliminated for those with gluten sensitivities.

1. Sort the beans, rinse well, and drain. In a 4- or 5-quart slow cooker, cover the beans with cool water. Let stand overnight.

2. In the morning, in a medium bowl, cover the dried porcini mushrooms with the warm water. Cover and let stand for 30 minutes.

3. Drain the mushrooms, reserving the soaking liquid. Strain the soaking liquid through cheesecloth to remove any grit.

4. Drain the beans, discarding the soaking liquid. In the slow cooker, stir well to combine the beans, soaked mushrooms, and their soaking liquid with the leek, fennel, Caramelized Onions, chopped onions, garlic, shiitake mushrooms, tomatoes, carrots, Veggie Broth, bay leaf, thyme, salt, and pepper.

5. Cover and cook on low for 8 to 10 hours, or until the beans and vegetables are tender.

6. Remove and discard the bay leaf.

7. In a large skillet, heat the olive oil. Add the bread crumbs, and toast over medium heat, stirring frequently, until the crumbs are crisp, about 5 minutes. Mix with the Parmesan cheese.

8. Serve the Cassoulet, garnished with the bread crumb mixture as desired.

2 cups dried cannellini beans

1 ounce dried porcini mushrooms

1 cup warm water

1 leek, chopped

1 fennel bulb, sliced

1 cup Caramelized Onions (page 181)

1 onion, chopped

3 garlic cloves, minced

2 cups sliced shiitake mushrooms

3 large tomatoes, seeded and chopped

4 carrots, sliced

4 cups Veggie Broth (page 60)

1 dried bay leaf

1 teaspoon dried thyme leaves

1 teaspoon salt

1/8 teaspoon freshly ground black pepper

3 tablespoons olive oil

3 cups soft whole-wheat bread crumbs

1 cup grated Parmesan cheese

BEAN *and* SPINACH ENCHILADA BAKE

SERVES: 6 • PREP TIME: 20 MINUTES
COOK TIME: 7 TO 9 HOURS ON LOW, PLUS 2 TO 5 MINUTES IN THE MICROWAVE

Canned beans are a great shortcut in this simple recipe, ensuring that they are tender by the end of the cooking time. This hearty and rich dish is perfect on a cold winter night. If preferred, substitute pinto or kidney beans for the black beans.

1. In a large bowl, mix to combine olive oil, onion, and garlic. Microwave on high for 2 to 5 minutes, stirring after 1 minute, until the vegetables are tender.

2. Add the poblano and jalapeño peppers, black beans, corn, tomatoes, tomatillos, tomato paste, chili powder, cumin, thyme, salt, and pepper to the bowl, and stir well.

3. In a medium bowl, mix to combine the salsa and tomato sauce.

4. In another medium bowl, mix to combine the Cheddar and Jack cheeses.

1 tablespoon olive oil

1 onion, chopped

4 garlic cloves, minced

1 poblano pepper, seeded and chopped

1 jalapeño pepper, minced

1 (16-ounce) can black beans, drained and rinsed

2 cups frozen corn

2 large tomatoes, seeded and chopped

2 tomatillos, peeled, rinsed, and chopped

3 tablespoons tomato paste

1 tablespoon chili powder

1 teaspoon ground cumin

1 teaspoon dried thyme leaves

1 teaspoon salt

⅛ teaspoon freshly ground black pepper

1½ cups salsa

1 (8-ounce) can tomato sauce

1 cup shredded Cheddar cheese

1 cup shredded Monterey Jack cheese

14 (6-inch) corn tortillas, softened according to package directions

5. Divide the bean mixture among the tortillas. Top each with some of the cheese mixture, and roll up.

6. In the bottom of a 4- or 5-quart slow cooker, put ¼ cup of the salsa mixture, and layer the filled tortillas on top, topping each with some of the salsa mixture before placing a rolled tortilla on top of another. Pour any remaining salsa mixture over the tortillas once they are all in the slow cooker.

7. Cover and cook on low for 7 to 9 hours, or until hot.

8. Carefully cut and scoop to serve.

Perfect Pair Serve enchiladas, as you would tacos or burritos, with additional shredded cheese, chopped tomatoes, salsa, avocados or guacamole, chopped green onions, and lettuce. These toppings add a cool component to the spicy peppers in the enchiladas and a texture contrast.

EGGPLANT LASAGNA

SERVES: 8 • PREP TIME: 20 MINUTES, PLUS 30 MINUTES TO STAND
COOK TIME: 7 TO 9 HOURS ON LOW, PLUS 5 TO 9 MINUTES ON THE STOVE TOP

Eggplant should be salted and rinsed before cooking. The salt extracts moisture from the eggplant that would otherwise be released while it cooks, which would make the recipe watery.

1. On 2 wire racks placed on rimmed baking sheets, sprinkle the eggplant slices with 1 teaspoon of salt. Turn the eggplant slices over, and sprinkle with the remaining 1 teaspoon of salt. Let stand for 30 minutes.

2. Press down on the eggplant slices lightly with your hands to remove more liquid.

3. Discard liquid from the baking sheets, rinse the eggplant slices, and pat dry.

4. In a heavy skillet, over medium heat, heat the olive oil; add the onions and garlic, and cook for 5 to 9 minutes, or until tender.

5. Stir in the red bell pepper, marjoram, oregano, and pasta sauce. Remove the pan from the heat.

6. In a medium bowl, mix well to combine the ricotta, eggs, black pepper, and cayenne pepper.

7. In the bottom of a 4-or 5-quart slow cooker, put about 1 cup of the pasta sauce mixture. Layer with one-third of the eggplant slices, followed by one-third of the ricotta mixture, one-third of the mozzarella, and one-third of the Parmesan. Repeat the layers, ending with the Parmesan.

8. Cover and cook on low for 7 to 9 hours, or until the eggplant is tender. Carefully cut and scoop to serve, topping with more Parmesan if desired.

2 large eggplant, sliced ½-inch thick crosswise

2 teaspoons salt, divided

2 tablespoons olive oil

2 onions, chopped

4 garlic cloves, sliced

1 red bell pepper, seeded and chopped

1 teaspoon dried marjoram leaves

1 teaspoon dried oregano leaves

1 (26-ounce) jar vegetarian pasta sauce

2 cups ricotta cheese

2 eggs

⅛ teaspoon freshly ground black pepper

⅛ teaspoon ground cayenne pepper

2 cups shredded mozzarella cheese, divided

½ cup shredded Parmesan cheese, divided

BARBECUE TOFU *and* BEANS

SERVES: 6 • PREP TIME: 15 MINUTES • COOK TIME: 8 TO 10 HOURS ON LOW

Tofu, a soy product, and beans, which are legumes, together provide complete protein. The combination is very satisfying and hearty, too. When you buy barbecue sauce, check the label, as not all are vegetarian, gluten-free, or soy-free.

1. Drain the tofu, and place it between paper towels. Press down on the tofu to remove most of the water. Cut into 1-inch cubes.

2. In a 4- or 5-quart slow cooker, stir well to combine the onions, garlic, jalapeño, chipotle chiles, adobo sauce, barbecue sauce, tomato paste, black beans, chickpeas, Veggie Broth, chili powder, salt, and pepper.

3. Cover and cook on low for 8 to 10 hours, or until the beans are tender.

4. Stir gently and serve.

1 pound firm tofu

2 onions, chopped

4 garlic cloves, sliced

1 jalapeño pepper, minced

2 chipotle chiles in adobo sauce, minced

3 tablespoons adobo sauce

1½ cups store-bought barbecue sauce

3 tablespoons tomato paste

1 (15-ounce) can black beans, drained and rinsed

1 (15-ounce) can chickpeas, drained and rinsed

4 cups Veggie Broth (page 60)

1 tablespoon chili powder

1 teaspoon salt

⅛ teaspoon freshly ground black pepper

TEX-MEX CASSEROLE

SERVES: 8 • PREP TIME: 25 MINUTES • COOK TIME: 7 TO 8 HOURS ON LOW

On a cold and rainy night, warmth and comfort are on the menu. Refried beans, soy crumbles, lots of vegetables, and tortilla chips are layered in a hearty casserole that is rich with spicy flavor. Tuck in with your favorite movie afterward, and your night is complete.

1. In a large bowl, mix to combine the onion, garlic, jalapeños, black beans, soy crumbles, and corn.

2. In a medium bowl, mix to combine the refried beans, salsa, tomato sauce, chili powder, cumin, salt, and pepper.

3. In the bottom of a 4- or 5-quart slow cooker, put 1 cup of the refried bean mixture. Top with one-third of the tortilla chips, then one-third of the soy crumble mixture, and one-third of the Cheddar and Pepper Jack cheeses. Repeat the tortilla chip, bean, and cheese layers, ending with the cheeses.

4. Cover and cook on low for 7 to 8 hours, or until the casserole is bubbling.

5. Carefully cut and scoop to serve.

1 onion, chopped

5 garlic cloves, minced

2 jalapeño peppers, minced

1 (15-ounce) can black beans, drained and rinsed

1 (12-ounce) package meatless soy crumbles, thawed

2 cups frozen corn

1 (15-ounce) can vegetarian refried beans

2 cups salsa

1 (8-ounce) can tomato sauce

1 tablespoon chili powder

1 teaspoon ground cumin

1 teaspoon salt

⅛ teaspoon freshly ground black pepper

4 cups tortilla chips, divided

2 cups shredded Cheddar cheese, divided

2 cups shredded Pepper Jack cheese, divided

LENTIL PASTITSIO

SERVES: 8 • PREP TIME: 25 MINUTES
COOK TIME: 8 TO 9 HOURS ON LOW, PLUS 30 TO 40 MINUTES ON HIGH

Pastitsio is a Greek casserole made of a meat sauce layered with pasta, then baked with a white sauce and cheese on top. The cinnamon gives it some of its unique flavor and is definitely an eye-popper. This recipe is transformed into a slow cooker meal with lentils, a sour cream sauce, and a much simpler preparation.

1. Sort the lentils, rinse well, and drain.

2. In a 5-quart slow cooker, stir well to combine the lentils, onion, garlic, diced tomatoes, tomato sauce, Veggie Broth, water, pasta, marjoram, oregano, thyme, cinnamon, salt, and pepper.

3. Cover and cook on low for 8 to 9 hours, or until the pasta is almost tender.

4. Stir the mixture in the slow cooker gently, and even out the top with the back of a spoon.

5. In a medium bowl, mix to combine the sour cream, ricotta, egg, cornstarch, nutmeg, and ¾ cup Parmesan cheese.

6. Pour the sour cream mixture over the pasta mixture in the slow cooker, spreading evenly. Sprinkle the remaining ¼ cup Parmesan cheese over the top.

7. Cover and cook on high for another 30 to 40 minutes, or until the sour cream mixture is set.

8. Turn off the slow cooker, and let stand for 20 minutes.

9. Scoop out carefully and serve.

1 cup green lentils

1 onion, chopped

3 garlic cloves, minced

1 (14-ounce) can diced tomatoes, undrained

1 (8-ounce) can tomato sauce

4 cups Veggie Broth (page 60)

2 cups water

1 (16-ounce) box whole-wheat penne or ziti

1 teaspoon dried marjoram leaves

½ teaspoon dried oregano leaves

½ teaspoon dried thyme leaves

½ teaspoon ground cinnamon

1 teaspoon salt

¼ teaspoon freshly ground black pepper

1 cup sour cream

1 cup ricotta cheese

1 egg

1 tablespoon cornstarch

Pinch ground nutmeg

1 cup grated Parmesan cheese, divided

BARBECUE TEMPEH

SERVES: 6 TO 8 • PREP TIME: 15 MINUTES • COOK TIME: 8 TO 10 HOURS ON LOW

This recipe is kind of like quasi-spare ribs. The texture of tempeh is similar to slow cooked meat. You can make this recipe spicy or mild, depending on the ingredients you use and your personal taste. But spicy or mild, it's tangy and delicious.

1. Cut the tempeh into 1-inch cubes.

2. In a 4- or 5-quart slow cooker, stir well to combine the onion, garlic, red bell peppers, chipotle chiles, adobo sauce, tomato sauce, ketchup, mustard, tomato paste, honey, maple syrup, vinegar, soy sauce, oregano, salt, and pepper. Stir in the tempeh cubes.

3. Cover and cook on low for 8 to 10 hours, or until the sauce is bubbling.

4. Stir gently and serve.

Serve this recipe over hot cooked grits, rice, or even mashed potatoes to soak up the wonderful sauce.

3 (8-ounce) packages tempeh

2 onions, chopped

4 garlic cloves, minced

2 red bell peppers, seeded and chopped

3 chipotle chiles in adobo sauce, minced

3 tablespoons adobo sauce

2 (8-ounce) cans tomato sauce

½ cup ketchup

3 tablespoons Dijon mustard

3 tablespoons tomato paste

¼ cup honey

2 tablespoons maple syrup

3 tablespoons apple cider vinegar

1 tablespoon soy sauce

1 teaspoon dried oregano leaves

1 teaspoon salt

⅛ teaspoon freshly ground black pepper

STRAIGHT-UP VEGETABLES

SPICY CORN ON THE COB

SERVES: 8 TO 10 • PREP TIME: 15 MINUTES • COOK TIME: 3 HOURS ON HIGH

Fresh corn on the cob is one of the best foods of summer. Nothing beats the crisp, sweet kernels. Cooking it in the slow cooker makes it even sweeter and more tender. The spicy coating on the corn is a nice contrast.

1. Pull the silk and leaves off the corn and discard.

2. In a small bowl, mix to combine the chili powder, chipotle powder, salt, black pepper, and cayenne pepper. Add the olive oil and lime juice, and mix well.

3. Rub this mixture onto the corn. Using a very sharp knife, cut each corn cob into 4 pieces. In a 5-quart slow cooker, pour the Veggie Broth in over the corn.

4. Cover and cook on high for 3 hours, or until the corn is tender.

5. Serve with the lime wedges on the side.

8 ears fresh corn

1 tablespoon chili powder

1 teaspoon dried chipotle powder

½ teaspoon salt

⅛ teaspoon freshly ground black pepper

⅛ teaspoon ground cayenne pepper

1 tablespoon olive oil

1 tablespoon freshly squeezed lime juice

1 cup Veggie Broth (page 60)

Lime wedges, for garnish

The Next Day This corn is wonderful turned into a soup the next day. Just cut the corn kernels off the cob, purée them with some vegetable broth or milk, and heat it on the stove top. Top with chopped green onions.

HERBED MASHED CAULIFLOWER

SERVES: 6 TO 8 • PREP TIME: 15 MINUTES • COOK TIME: 7 TO 8 HOURS ON LOW

Cauliflower has replaced potatoes in this classic mashed dish, beloved as the ultimate comfort food. Not only does this recipe taste very much like mashed potatoes, it's high in antioxidants and fiber. Bring on the mashed goodness!

1. Remove the leaves from the cauliflower and discard. Cut the florets off the cauliflower. Cut the stems into 1-inch pieces.

2. In a 4- or 5-quart slow cooker, stir well to combine the cauliflower, leek, garlic, Veggie Broth, thyme, salt, and pepper.

3. Cover and cook on low for 7 to 8 hours, or until the cauliflower is very tender.

4. Remove and discard the thyme stems. Stir the butter, cream, chives, and parsley into the slow cooker.

5. Purée the cauliflower right in the slow cooker using an immersion blender or potato masher, or purée in batches in a food processor or blender, and serve.

2 large heads cauliflower

1 leek, chopped

3 garlic cloves, minced

1 cup Veggie Broth (page 60)

2 fresh thyme sprigs

1 teaspoon salt

1/8 teaspoon freshly ground black pepper

1/3 cup butter or olive oil

1 cup light cream or almond milk

2 tablespoons minced fresh chives

3 tablespoons minced fresh flat-leaf parsley

CREAMY MUSHROOM HASH BROWNS

SERVES: 8 • PREP TIME: 15 MINUTES
COOK TIME: 6 TO 8 HOURS ON LOW, PLUS 20 TO 30 MINUTES ON HIGH

You can make your own hash brown potatoes by grating the potatoes, either in a food processor or on a hand grater, but the frozen varieties are of very high quality and much easier to use. This comforting side dish is excellent in the winter.

1. In a 4- or 5-quart slow cooker, stir well to combine the frozen hash browns, onions, mushrooms, and garlic.

2. Pour the Veggie Broth and olive oil over the vegetables, and sprinkle with the tarragon, salt, and pepper.

3. Cover and cook on low for 6 to 8 hours, or until the vegetables are tender.

4. Stir in the cream cheese, ricotta, and sour cream. Cover and cook on high for another 20 to 30 minutes, or until the mixture is thickened and bubbly.

5. Stir gently and serve.

1 (30-ounce) package frozen hash brown potatoes

2 onions, chopped

2 cups sliced cremini or shiitake mushrooms

4 garlic cloves, minced

1 cup Veggie Broth (page 60)

3 tablespoons olive oil

1 teaspoon dried tarragon leaves

1 teaspoon salt

⅛ teaspoon freshly ground black pepper

1 (8-ounce) package cream cheese, cut into cubes

1 cup ricotta cheese

1 cup sour cream

Prep It Right

If you are at home during the day, stir this recipe a few times while it's cooking. That way the brown bits on the sides of the slow cooker will mix into the center and add that much more great flavor.

SPAGHETTI SQUASH

SERVES: 6 • PREP TIME: 10 MINUTES • COOK TIME: 7 TO 8 HOURS ON LOW

Spaghetti squash is a fabulous substitute for spaghetti or linguine. This unusual vegetable's flesh cooks into long strands that really have the texture of cooked pasta. Make sure that the spaghetti squash will fit into your slow cooker before you begin.

2 small spaghetti squash

⅓ cup water

2 tablespoons butter or olive oil

1 teaspoon dried thyme leaves

1 teaspoon salt

⅓ teaspoon freshly ground black pepper

1. Pierce the squash with a sharp knife in a few places so it doesn't explode in the slow cooker. In a 4- to 6-quart slow cooker, cover the squash with the water.

2. Cover and cook on low for 7 to 8 hours, or until the squash is very tender.

3. Carefully remove the squash from the slow cooker, and let it cool for 10 minutes.

4. Carefully cut the squash in half and remove the seeds. Scrape out the flesh, which will have separated into strands. Drain if necessary.

5. In a serving bowl, gently toss the squash strands with the butter, thyme, salt, and pepper, and serve.

Perfect Pair Serve this recipe with any of the savory sauces in this book for a great dinner. Make the sauces the day before and refrigerate. Then reheat on the stove top when you get home, prepare the cooked squash, and eat.

CREAMY SQUASH *and* VEGGIES

SERVES: 8 • PREP TIME: 25 MINUTES
COOK TIME: 8 HOURS, 15 MINUTES TO 10 HOURS, 20 MINUTES ON LOW

Silken tofu and coconut milk are the secret ingredients in this creamy casserole. Silken tofu is just that—silky and creamy, and very much like sour cream. If you're a vegan who's been missing the texture sour cream can bring to veggies, this is your dish.

1. In a 4- or 5-quart slow cooker, stir well to combine the butternut squash, acorn squash, onion, fennel, garlic, carrots, Veggie Broth, rosemary, salt, and pepper.

2. Cover and cook on low for 8 to 10 hours, or until vegetables are tender.

3. In a blender or food processor, process the silken tofu and coconut milk until smooth. Stir the mixture into the slow cooker.

4. Cover and cook on low for another 15 to 20 minutes, or until the sauce is hot.

5. Stir gently and serve.

The Next Day Any vegetable mixture—this one included—is delicious served as bruschetta the next day. Just toast some bread, spread with butter or drizzle with olive oil, and top with the cooked vegetables. Add some cheese if you'd like, and then broil until hot and bubbly.

3 cups peeled, seeded, and cubed butternut squash

3 cups peeled, seeded, and cubed acorn squash

2 onions, chopped

1 fennel bulb, chopped

3 garlic cloves, minced

3 carrots, peeled and sliced

2 cups Veggie Broth (page 60)

1 sprig fresh rosemary

1 teaspoon salt

⅛ teaspoon freshly ground black pepper

1 (12-ounce) package silken tofu

½ cup coconut milk

POTATO-BEAN SALAD

SERVES: 6 • PREP TIME: 25 MINUTES, PLUS OVERNIGHT TO SOAK AND OVERNIGHT TO CHILL
COOK TIME: 8 TO 10 HOURS ON LOW

Using your slow cooker to prepare a main dish salad saves a lot of time. The food cooks all day, and then you mix it with a dressing and refrigerate overnight. Voila! Dinner is ready for the next couple of days.

1. Sort the black and navy beans, rinse well, and drain. In a 4- or 5-quart slow cooker, cover the beans with cool water. Let stand overnight.

2. In the morning, drain the beans, discarding the soaking liquid.

3. Cut the potatoes into 1½-inch cubes.

4. In the slow cooker, stir well to combine the beans, potatoes, onion, garlic, Veggie Broth, and 1 teaspoon of salt.

5. Cover and cook on low for 8 to 10 hours, or until the beans and potatoes are tender.

6. In a very large bowl, mix well to combine the mayonnaise, yogurt, mustard, lemon juice, honey, marjoram, thyme, pepper, and the remaining ½ teaspoon of salt. Stir in the red bell peppers.

7. Transfer the vegetables and beans from the slow cooker, draining them as you go, to the bowl with the dressing. Discard any remaining liquid in the slow cooker.

8. Stir the salad gently to coat, cover, and refrigerate overnight before serving.

1 cup dried black beans

1 cup dried navy beans

8 large russet potatoes, peeled

2 onions, chopped

3 garlic cloves, minced

5 cups Veggie Broth (page 60)

1½ teaspoons salt, divided

1 cup mayonnaise

1 cup Greek yogurt

¼ cup Dijon mustard

3 tablespoons freshly squeezed lemon juice

2 tablespoons honey

1 teaspoon dried marjoram leaves

1 teaspoon dried thyme leaves

⅛ teaspoon freshly ground black pepper

2 red bell peppers, seeded and chopped

CARAMELIZED ONION MASHED POTATOES

SERVES: 6 • PREP TIME: 25 MINUTES • COOK TIME: 8 TO 10 HOURS ON LOW

Who knew mashed potatoes could be even more perfect? With the deep and rich flavors of caramelized onion added, you won't want to eat mashed potatoes any other way. There's a reason why the Caramelized Onions (page 181) make so much—there are so many great ways to use them. These mashed potatoes are just one of them.

5 pounds russet potatoes, peeled and cubed

2 cups Caramelized Onions (page 181)

1 onion, sliced

6 garlic cloves

1 cup Veggie Broth (page 60)

1 ½ teaspoons salt

⅛ teaspoon freshly ground white pepper

½ cup butter

1 cup light cream

¼ cup minced chives

2 tablespoons minced fresh flat-leaf parsley

1. In a 5-quart slow cooker, stir well to combine the potatoes, Caramelized Onions, sliced onions, garlic, Veggie Broth, salt, and white pepper.

2. Cover and cook on low until the potatoes are very tender, 8 to 10 hours.

3. Stir in the butter. In the slow cooker, mash the potatoes using a potato masher, adding enough cream so the potatoes reach your desired consistency.

4. Stir in the chives and parsley and serve.

Prep It Right

You can make these mashed potatoes three to four hours ahead of the time you want to serve them. Just keep the slow cooker covered and set on "keep warm."

RATATOUILLE

SERVES: 6 TO 8 • PREP TIME: 20 MINUTES, PLUS 30 MINUTES TO STAND
COOK TIME: 6 TO 8 HOURS ON LOW

Ratatouille is a classic French stew that is rich with vegetables and beans. It makes an excellent side dish, or it can be a main dish when served with some toasted bread and a green salad. Whichever way you serve it, it's vegetable heaven.

1. Cut the eggplant into 1-inch cubes. In a large colander or strainer in the sink, sprinkle 1 teaspoon of salt over the eggplant. Let stand for 30 minutes.

2. Rinse the eggplant, and drain well; pat dry with paper towels.

3. In a 5-quart slow cooker, stir well to combine the eggplant, onions, garlic, mushrooms, bell peppers, summer squash, tomatoes, tomato paste, honey, lemon juice, bay leaf, thyme, marjoram, pepper, and the remaining ½ teaspoon salt.

4. Cover and cook on low for 6 to 8 hours, or until the vegetables are tender.

5. Remove and discard the thyme stems and bay leaf, stir gently, and serve.

- 1 large eggplant, peeled
- 1½ teaspoons salt, divided
- 2 onions, chopped
- 5 garlic cloves, minced
- 2 cups sliced cremini mushrooms
- 2 red bell peppers, seeded and chopped
- 2 yellow summer squash, chopped
- 5 large tomatoes, seeded and chopped
- 1 (6-ounce) can tomato paste
- 1 tablespoon honey
- 1 tablespoon freshly squeezed lemon juice
- 1 dried bay leaf
- 2 fresh thyme sprigs
- 1 teaspoon dried marjoram leaves
- ⅛ teaspoon freshly ground black pepper

The Next Day

Leftover ratatouille makes a great pizza. Spread the mixture on a prepared pizza crust, top with cheese, and bake at 400°F for 15 to 20 minutes, or until hot.

EGGPLANT PARMESAN CASSEROLE

SERVES: 6 • PREP TIME: 20 MINUTES, PLUS 30 MINUTES TO STAND
COOK TIME: 7 TO 9 HOURS ON LOW, PLUS 5 MINUTES ON THE STOVE TOP

Typical eggplant Parmesan is usually made from slices of eggplant, coated in egg and breadcrumbs, and deep-fried. When made in the slow cooker, it's much better for you and just as tasty. Because the breadcrumbs would get soggy in the slow cooker, they are saved and sprinkled on top just before serving.

1 large eggplant, peeled and cubed

1½ teaspoons salt, divided

1 onion, chopped

2 cups sliced shiitake mushrooms

3 large tomatoes, seeded and chopped

3 garlic cloves, sliced

1 cup Marinara Sauce (page 65)

3 tablespoons tomato paste

1 teaspoon dried oregano leaves

1 teaspoon dried thyme leaves

1 teaspoon dried basil leaves

⅛ teaspoon freshly ground black pepper

1½ cups shredded Parmesan cheese, divided

1½ cups soft breadcrumbs

3 tablespoons extra-virgin olive oil

1. Cut the eggplant into 1-inch cubes. In a large colander or strainer in the sink, sprinkle 1 teaspoon of salt over the eggplant. Let stand for 30 minutes.

2. Rinse the eggplant, and drain well; pat dry with paper towels.

3. In a 4- or 5-quart slow cooker, stir well to combine the eggplant, onion, mushrooms, tomatoes, garlic, Marinara Sauce, tomato paste, oregano, thyme, basil, pepper, and the remaining ½ teaspoon of salt.

4. Cover and cook on low for 7 to 9 hours, or until the vegetables are tender. Stir in 1 cup of the Parmesan cheese, and then sprinkle the top with the remaining ½ cup cheese.

5. In a small saucepan over medium-high heat, toast the breadcrumbs in the olive oil, stirring frequently, until crisp, about 5 minutes.

6. Sprinkle the breadcrumbs over each serving of the casserole.

SPICED ROASTED ROOT VEGGIES

SERVES: 8 TO 10 • PREP TIME: 30 MINUTES • COOK TIME: 6 TO 8 HOURS ON LOW

Root vegetables are delicious with all kinds of herbs, but have you ever had them roasted with spices? These warm spices add a wonderful richness to this recipe. It's a wonderful and unexpected way to prepare root vegetables.

1. In a 4- or 5-quart slow cooker, stir well to combine the potatoes, sweet potatoes, carrots, parsnips, onions, garlic, olive oil, maple syrup, salt, cinnamon, cumin, nutmeg, cloves, black pepper, and cayenne pepper.

2. Cover and cook on low for 6 to 8 hours, or until the vegetables are tender.

3. Stir gently and serve.

The Next Day Turn these roasted root vegetables into a salad the next day. Toss them with lots of different kinds of lettuces and toasted nuts, and drizzle with your favorite salad dressing.

4 russet potatoes, peeled and cubed

2 sweet potatoes, peeled and cubed

4 carrots, sliced

2 parsnips, peeled and cubed

2 onions, chopped

10 garlic cloves

2 tablespoons olive oil

3 tablespoons maple syrup

1 teaspoon salt

½ teaspoon ground cinnamon

1 teaspoon ground cumin

¼ teaspoon ground nutmeg

⅛ teaspoon ground cloves

⅛ teaspoon freshly ground black pepper

⅛ teaspoon ground cayenne pepper

COUNTRY VEGETABLE BAKE

SERVES: 6 TO 8 • PREP TIME: 25 MINUTES
COOK TIME: 8 HOURS, 20 MINUTES TO 10 HOURS, 30 MINUTES ON LOW

This colorful and rich side dish is full of fiber and numerous healthy nutrients, including vitamin A. I served it as part of our Thanksgiving dinner last year and received so many requests for the recipe, I made it for Christmas, too!

1. In a 4-quart slow cooker, stir well to combine the potatoes, carrots, leek, Veggie Broth, thyme, marjoram, salt, and pepper.

2. Cover and cook on low for 8 to 10 hours, or until the vegetables are tender.

3. Stir in the peas, and then cover and cook on low for another 20 to 30 minutes, or until the peas are tender.

4. Stir gently and serve.

5 russet potatoes, peeled and cut into chunks

4 large carrots, sliced

1 leek, chopped

1 cup Veggie Broth (page 60)

2 fresh thyme sprigs

1 teaspoon dried marjoram leaves

1 teaspoon salt

1/8 teaspoon freshly ground black pepper

2 cups frozen baby peas

TEX-MEX VEGETABLES

SERVES: 6 • PREP TIME: 25 MINUTES • COOK TIME: 6 TO 7 HOURS ON LOW

Sometimes all you want is some nice vegetables, roasted with lots of spices, to serve over mashed potatoes or polenta. This spicy blend is perfect for a cold winter evening. Mashed potatoes or polenta provide a creamy palate soother to the Tex-Mex flavors.

1. In a 4- or 5-quart slow cooker, stir well to combine the red, yellow, orange, and green bell peppers with the onion, garlic, jalapeños, Veggie Broth, olive oil, chili powder, oregano, salt, black pepper, and cayenne pepper.

2. Cover and cook on low for 6 to 7 hours, or until the vegetables are very tender. You can cook this recipe longer if you'd like, up to 9 to 10 hours, as long as you are home to stir the vegetables after 7 hours.

3. Stir gently and serve.

2 red bell peppers, seeded and thickly sliced

2 yellow bell peppers, seeded and thickly sliced

2 orange bell peppers, seeded and thickly sliced

2 green bell peppers, seeded and thickly sliced

3 onions, sliced

8 garlic cloves, sliced

2 jalapeño peppers, sliced

½ cup Veggie Broth (page 60)

1 tablespoon olive oil

1 tablespoon chili powder

1 teaspoon dried oregano leaves

1 teaspoon salt

⅛ teaspoon freshly ground black pepper

⅛ teaspoon ground cayenne pepper

ROASTED GARLIC MASHED ROOT VEGGIES

SERVES: 6 TO 8 • PREP TIME: 25 MINUTES • COOK TIME: 8 TO 10 HOURS ON LOW

If you want to try something different from mashed potatoes or even mashed cauliflower, why not mash a medley of root vegetables? The garlic in this recipe is used in three ways: whole, sliced, and minced. These preparations change the flavor of the garlic as it's cooked—whole stays sweet, sliced is more pungent, and the minced garlic spreads the flavor around the whole dish.

1 celery root, peeled and cubed

4 carrots, peeled and sliced

2 onions, chopped

5 whole garlic cloves

5 garlic cloves, sliced

5 garlic cloves, minced

2 parsnips, peeled and cubed

2 sweet potatoes, peeled and cubed

½ cup Veggie Broth (page 60)

1 teaspoon salt

1 teaspoon dried thyme leaves

⅛ teaspoon freshly ground black pepper

⅓ cup extra-virgin olive oil

1. In a 4- or 5-quart slow cooker, stir well to combine the celery root, carrots, onions, garlic cloves, garlic slices, minced garlic, parsnips, sweet potatoes, Veggie Broth, salt, thyme, and pepper.

2. Cover and cook on low for 8 to 10 hours, or until all the vegetables are very tender.

3. Drizzle the olive oil all over everything, and mash the vegetables, using an immersion blender or potato masher, right in the slow cooker. Taste for seasoning and serve.

Substitute Tip

You can vary this recipe as you'd like, using your favorite root veggies. Try Jerusalem artichokes, rutabagas, russet potatoes, or Yukon Gold potatoes for a change of pace.

GERMAN POTATO SALAD

SERVES: 6 TO 8 • PREP TIME: 25 MINUTES • COOK TIME: 7 TO 9 HOURS ON LOW,
PLUS 15 TO 20 MINUTES ON HIGH

German potato salad is always served hot, which makes it different from regular mayonnaise-based potato salads. I like using mushrooms and caramelized onions to add even more great flavor, and add some cabbage for color and texture.

1. In a 4-quart slow cooker, stir well to combine the potatoes, onions, garlic, cabbage, Veggie Broth, salt, dill seed, and pepper.

2. Cover and cook on low for 7 to 9 hours, or until the vegetables are tender.

3. In a medium bowl, mix well to combine the vinegar, lemon juice, mustard, cornstarch, honey, and sour cream. Stir the sour cream mixture into the slow cooker.

4. Cover and cook on high for 15 to 20 minutes longer, or until the sauce has thickened.

5. Serve warm.

8 russet potatoes, peeled and cubed

2 onions, chopped

4 garlic cloves, minced

4 cups chopped purple cabbage

1 cup Veggie Broth (page 60)

1 teaspoon salt

1 teaspoon dill seed

1/8 teaspoon freshly ground black pepper

2/3 cup apple cider vinegar

2 tablespoons freshly squeezed lemon juice

3 tablespoons grainy mustard

3 tablespoons cornstarch

1/3 cup honey

1 1/4 cups sour cream

Prep It Right

The vinegar dressing is added at the end of cooking time in this recipe; otherwise the acid in the dressing would prevent the potatoes from softening. Don't add the vinegar until the potatoes are cooked.

SWEET *and* SOUR BRUSSELS SPROUTS

SERVES: 8 • PREP TIME: 20 MINUTES • COOK TIME: 5 TO 7 HOURS ON LOW

Let's face it: You either love or hate Brussels sprouts. But even a Brussels sprouts hater can be converted to a lover with this recipe. The sprouts are cooked until they are soft, with a few flavorful brown bits, and the sweet and sour sauce is luscious.

1. Trim the edges of the Brussels sprouts.

2. In a 3- or 4-quart slow cooker, stir well to combine the Brussels sprouts, onion, garlic, ketchup, vinegar, lemon juice, honey, brown sugar, mustard, salt, and pepper.

3. Cover and cook on low for 5 to 7 hours, or until the sprouts are tender.

4. Stir gently and serve.

2 pounds Brussels sprouts

1 onion, chopped

4 garlic cloves, minced

½ cup ketchup

¼ cup apple cider vinegar

2 tablespoons freshly squeezed lemon juice

¼ cup honey

2 tablespoons brown sugar

2 tablespoons honey mustard

1 teaspoon salt

⅛ teaspoon freshly ground black pepper

CREAMY CABBAGE

SERVES: 8 • PREP TIME: 25 MINUTES
COOK TIME: 7 TO 9 HOURS ON LOW, PLUS 10 TO 20 MINUTES ON HIGH

Cabbage is such an inexpensive vegetable, and it pairs so well with so many flavors. This cruciferous vegetable is packed with fiber, glucosinolates that may help prevent cancer, and the nutrients manganese and vitamin C. Plus, it tastes great. What more can you ask for in a vegetable?

1 head red cabbage

1 head green cabbage

1 leek, peeled and chopped

3 garlic cloves, minced

½ cup Veggie Broth (page 60)

1 teaspoon salt

1 teaspoon dried dill weed

1 teaspoon dried thyme leaves

⅛ teaspoon freshly ground black pepper

1 (12-ounce) package silken tofu

2 tablespoons freshly squeezed lemon juice

2 tablespoons honey

1. Remove outer leaves of the red and green cabbages, and cut out the cores. Cut the cabbage into 1-inch pieces.

2. In a 4- or 5-quart slow cooker, stir well to combine the cabbage, leek, garlic, Veggie Broth, salt, dill, thyme, and pepper.

3. Cover and cook on low for 7 to 9 hours, or until the vegetables are tender.

4. In a blender or food processor, blend the tofu with the lemon juice and honey until smooth.

5. Stir the tofu mixture into the slow cooker, cover, and cook on high for 10 to 20 minutes longer, or until the sauce is hot.

 The Next Day

Turn this side dish into a soup. Add some Veggie Broth along with some cooked lentils or beans, and heat on the stove top until steaming.

ROASTED BEETS

SERVES: 8 • PREP TIME: 10 MINUTES • COOK TIME: 6 TO 8 HOURS ON LOW

Beets are packed with nutrients including vitamin C, potassium, B vitamins, and manganese. They are also delicious, especially when roasted with onions and honey. Beets can be messy to prepare, but when cooked in the slow cooker, the skins will slip right off.

4 pounds beets

1 onion, chopped

5 tablespoons olive oil

2 tablespoons honey

1 teaspoon dried thyme leaves

1 teaspoon salt

⅛ teaspoon freshly ground black pepper

1. Scrub the beets well, but do not peel them. Cut off all but 1 inch of the tops. Reserve the beet greens to use in another recipe.

2. In a sealable slow cooker liner, combine the beets, onion, olive oil, honey, thyme, salt, and pepper.

3. Close the liner, and put it in a 4- or 5-quart slow cooker. Cover and cook on low for 6 to 8 hours, or until the beets are tender.

4. Remove the liner from the slow cooker, and empty it into a large bowl. Let the beets cool until you can handle them.

5. Remove and discard the skins from the beets. You can mix the beets with some of the liquid remaining in the liner if you'd like, or just slice or chop the beets and dig in.

The Next Day These roasted beets can be used to make Borscht (page 95) or added to salads. Or just eat them plain, drizzled with more olive oil and honey.

MASHED TURNIPS *and* ONIONS

SERVES: 6 • PREP TIME: 15 MINUTES
COOK TIME: 6 HOURS, 15 MINUTES TO 8 HOURS, 20 MINUTES ON LOW

Turnips are an "old-fashioned" root vegetable that not many people use anymore. That's too bad, because they make a suave and velvety mash that's better than mashed potatoes, in my humble opinion. The turnips are cooked with three kinds of onions in this easy recipe.

4 pounds turnips

1 leek, chopped

2 onions, chopped

½ cup **Veggie Broth** (page 60)

1 teaspoon salt

⅛ teaspoon freshly ground black pepper

⅓ cup butter

3 tablespoons extra-virgin olive oil

1 cup light cream

3 tablespoons chopped chives

1. Scrub the turnips well and peel them. Chop into 1-inch pieces.

2. In a 4- or 5-quart slow cooker, stir well to combine the turnips, leek, onions, Veggie Broth, salt, and pepper.

3. Cover and cook on low for 6 to 8 hours, or until the vegetables are tender.

4. Add the butter and olive oil to the slow cooker. Mash the turnips right in the slow cooker with an immersion blender or potato masher. Add the cream, mash again, and stir in the chives.

5. Cover and cook on low for another 15 to 20 minutes, or until hot.

6. You can keep the mash warm for 2 to 3 hours before serving. Just turn the slow cooker to "keep warm."

CELERY ROOT-REMOULADE CASSEROLE

SERVES: 6 • PREP TIME: 15 MINUTES
COOK TIME: 6 HOURS, 20 MINUTES TO 8 HOURS, 30 MINUTES ON LOW

Celery root remoulade is typically made with raw celery root (also known as celeriac), cut into strips, and enveloped in a creamy dressing for a cold salad. This recipe turns that on its head and makes it into a casserole, adding lots of other veggies for color and interest.

1. Cut the celery roots into 1½-inch cubes. In a 4- or 5-quart slow cooker, stir well to combine the celery roots, carrots, celery, mushrooms, leek, garlic, Veggie Broth, salt, and pepper.

2. Cover and cook on low for 6 to 8 hours, or until the vegetables are tender.

3. Drain the vegetables, discarding the cooking liquid. Return the vegetables to the slow cooker, and stir in the tofu, mustard, and lemon juice.

4. Cover and cook on low for another 20 to 30 minutes, or until hot.

5. Sprinkle with the chives and serve.

- 4 celery roots, peeled
- 4 carrots, peeled and sliced
- 4 celery stalks, sliced
- 2 cups sliced mushrooms
- 1 leek, chopped
- 5 garlic cloves, minced
- ½ cup Veggie Broth (page 60)
- 1 teaspoon salt
- ⅛ teaspoon freshly ground black pepper
- 1 (12-ounce) package silken tofu
- ¼ cup Dijon mustard
- ¼ cup freshly squeezed lemon juice
- 3 tablespoons minced fresh chives

Ingredient Tip

Celery root looks intimidating. It's big and knobby and looks completely inedible, but it is suave and delicious, with a slight flavor of celery. Peel it using a sharp knife instead of a vegetable peeler.

MARINATED MUSHROOMS

SERVES: 6 • PREP TIME: 15 MINUTES • COOK TIME: 5 TO 7 HOURS ON LOW

Mushrooms readily absorb the flavors of whatever they are cooked with. They are natural sponges. This casserole is flavored with lots of herbs, mustard, and onion. It's delicious served hot or cold.

1. In a 4- or 5-quart slow cooker, stir well to combine the cremini, button, and shiitake mushrooms with the onions, garlic, Veggie Broth, olive oil, thyme, bay leaf, oregano, salt, and pepper.

2. Cover and cook on low for 5 to 7 hours, or until the mushrooms are tender.

3. Remove and discard the thyme stems and the bay leaf, stir gently, and serve.

2 cups whole cremini mushrooms

2 cups whole button mushrooms

2 cups whole shiitake mushrooms

2 onions, chopped

4 garlic cloves, minced

½ cup Veggie Broth (page 60)

2 tablespoons olive oil

2 fresh thyme sprigs

1 dried bay leaf

1 teaspoon dried oregano leaves

1 teaspoon salt

⅛ teaspoon freshly ground black pepper

CARAMELIZED ONIONS

MAKES 8 CUPS • PREP TIME: 15 MINUTES • COOK TIME: 12 HOURS ON LOW

Caramelized onions are an essential ingredient in many recipes, and the slow cooker is the perfect way to make them! These onions are cooked until they are deep golden brown. They add a rich and slightly sweet taste to recipes and are delicious served on their own.

4 onions, chopped

4 onions, sliced

¼ cup butter or olive oil

1 teaspoon sugar

1½ teaspoons salt

1. In a 3- or 4-quart slow cooker, stir well to combine the chopped and sliced onions, butter, sugar, and salt.

2. Cover and cook on low for 10 hours, or until the onions are soft and brown.

3. Stir the onions, partially cover the slow cooker, and cook for another 2 hours on low.

4. Stir the onions again.

5. Let the onions cool, and then refrigerate in an airtight container for up to 1 week or freeze for up to 3 months.

GARLICKY BRUSSELS SPROUTS *with* CHICKPEAS

SERVES: 6 • PREP TIME: 15 MINUTES • COOK TIME: 5 TO 7 HOURS ON LOW

Brussels sprouts are delicious when slowly roasted in the slow cooker with lots of garlic. If you really love garlic—there's never too much, in my opinion—add more!

1. Trim the edges of the Brussels sprouts. In a 3- or 4-quart slow cooker, stir well to combine the Brussels sprouts, sliced garlic, minced garlic, chickpeas, Veggie Broth, salt, pepper, and hazelnuts.

2. Cover and cook on low for 5 to 7 hours, or until the sprouts are tender.

3. Stir gently and serve.

2 pounds Brussels sprouts

8 garlic cloves, sliced

4 garlic cloves, minced

1 (15-ounce) can chickpeas, drained and rinsed

½ cup Veggie Broth (page 60)

1 teaspoon salt

⅛ teaspoon freshly ground black pepper

1 cup chopped hazelnuts

LEMONY ARTICHOKES

SERVES: 6 • PREP TIME: 30 MINUTES • COOK TIME: 5 TO 7 HOURS ON LOW

Whoever first decided an artichoke was edible was a brave person. You eat this vegetable by pulling off individual leaves and scraping out the flesh with your teeth. Preparing an artichoke takes time, but the taste is well worth it. While you can boil artichokes, using the slow cooker to make them is even easier and takes the guesswork out of cooking them.

2 cups Veggie Broth (page 60)

1 cup water

1 lemon, sliced and seeded

3 tablespoons freshly squeezed lemon juice

4 garlic cloves

1 teaspoon salt

1 teaspoon dried marjoram leaves

⅛ teaspoon freshly ground black pepper

6 large artichokes

1. In a 4- or 5-quart slow cooker, stir well to combine the Veggie Broth, water, lemon slices, lemon juice, garlic, salt, marjoram, and pepper.

2. To prepare the artichokes, rinse them well. Then use a sharp knife to cut off the top 1 inch of each artichoke. Trim and peel the stem, removing the tough skin, and pull off any discolored leaves. Then cut off the thorns on the top of the leaves with kitchen shears.

3. Open each artichoke, using your fingers, and remove the "choke," which is the fuzzy center that sits on top of the artichoke heart. As you do this with each artichoke, add the artichoke to the liquid in the slow cooker to prevent it from browning.

4. Cover and cook on low for 5 to 7 hours, or until you can easily pull a leaf out of the artichoke.

5. Remove the artichokes from the slow cooker, and drain them upside down on kitchen towels.

6. Serve warm.

Serve artichokes with melted butter with some garlic or mustard added, or with olive oil mixed with herbs. You can also serve this vegetable with mayonnaise or silken tofu mixed with some mustard and chopped green onion.

BRAISED DARK GREENS

SERVES: 8 TO 10 • PREP TIME: 15 MINUTES, PLUS 30 MINUTES TO SOAK
COOK TIME: 6 HOURS ON LOW, PLUS 15 MINUTES ON THE STOVE TOP

Collard greens are so good for you, with lots of vitamins A and C. They can be bitter, but when cooked for a long time with lots of seasonings, they are tender, velvety, and delicious. They are usually cooked with ham or bacon, but we'll use caramelized onions and mushrooms.

1. In a medium bowl, cover the dried mushrooms with the warm water. Let stand for 30 minutes.

2. Drain the mushrooms, reserving the soaking liquid. Strain the soaking liquid through cheesecloth to remove any grit. Remove and discard the mushroom stems if they are tough, and chop the mushrooms.

3. Sort the collard, beet, and mustard greens and kale, removing any torn or bruised leaves. Cut the tough stems out of the kale. Clean the greens by immersing them in a sink full of cold water. Change the water a few times, swishing the greens with your hands, until any grit and sand is gone. Roughly chop all of the greens.

1 ounce dried morel mushrooms

1 cup warm water

2 pounds collard greens

1 pound beet greens

1 pound mustard greens

1 pound kale

1 cup Caramelized Onions (page 181)

1 onion, chopped

5 garlic cloves, minced

2 cups sliced cremini mushrooms

1 cup Veggie Broth (page 60)

1 teaspoon salt

1 teaspoon dried marjoram leaves

⅛ teaspoon freshly ground black pepper

4. Bring a large pot of water to a boil. Add one-quarter of the greens, and cook for a few minutes, just until wilted. (This is the only way to get the greens to fit into the slow cooker.) Transfer the wilted greens to a colander in the sink to drain. Occasionally press down on the greens in the colander with a ladle or the back of a spoon to remove excess water. Continue to do this until all the greens are wilted and drained.

5. In a 4- or 5-quart slow cooker, stir well to combine the wilted and drained greens, dried mushrooms, mushroom soaking liquid, Caramelized Onions, chopped onions, garlic, cremini mushrooms, Veggie Broth, salt, marjoram, and pepper.

6. Cover and cook on low for 6 hours, or until the greens are very tender.

7. Stir gently and serve.

The liquid that remains after you cook the greens is called "pot liquor." It's a delicious broth and can be used in soup or to dip cornbread in.

BREAKFASTS

CHAPTER NINE

PUMPKIN-APPLE BREAKFAST BARS

SERVES: 6 • PREP TIME: 25 MINUTES • COOK TIME: 6 TO 7 HOURS ON LOW

Yes, you can make breakfast bars in the slow cooker! These bars are very moist and tender because of the slow cooking temperature and environment. This recipe is full of texture and flavor, and these bars are a great way to start your day full of energy.

1 cup solid-pack pumpkin purée (not pumpkin pie filling)

2 eggs

2 teaspoons vanilla

1 cup milk

½ cup apple juice

2 cups old-fashioned oatmeal

1 Granny Smith apple, peeled, cored, and finely chopped

½ cup raisins

⅓ cup almond flour

1 teaspoon ground cinnamon

1 teaspoon baking powder

¼ teaspoon salt

Nonstick spray

1 cup chopped walnuts

1. In a large bowl, mix well to combine the pumpkin purée and eggs. Stir in the vanilla, milk, and apple juice, and then stir in the oatmeal, apple, raisins, almond flour, cinnamon, baking powder, and salt.

2. Prepare a 6-quart slow cooker by lining it with an aluminum foil sling, then with parchment paper. Spray the parchment paper with the nonstick spray.

3. Spread the batter into the slow cooker, and sprinkle with the chopped walnuts.

4. Cover and cook on low for 6 to 7 hours, or until the bars are almost firm when touched.

5. Turn the slow cooker off, and let cool for 1 hour.

6. Using the foil sling, lift the bars out of the slow cooker to cool on a wire rack. Cut into bars and serve.

WHOLE-GRAIN PORRIDGE

SERVES: 8 • PREP TIME: 15 MINUTES • COOK TIME: 7 TO 9 HOURS ON LOW

Orange juice provides a fresh flavor in this multigrain hot cereal recipe. Add a drizzle of some cold cream on top for a wonderful contrast. Drizzle or not, a breakfast chock-full of fiber, potassium, and iron is a perfect way to start your day and keep you energized.

- ½ cup wild rice
- ½ cup wheat berries
- ¾ cup hulled barley
- ¾ cup steel-cut oats
- ⅔ cup dried cranberries
- 3 tablespoons honey
- 2 tablespoons brown sugar
- 1 cup freshly squeezed orange juice
- 7 cups water
- ½ teaspoon salt

1. In a 4- or 5-quart slow cooker, stir well to combine the wild rice, wheat berries, barley, oats, cranberries, honey, brown sugar, orange juice, water, and salt.

2. Cover and cook on low for 7 to 9 hours, or until the grains are tender.

3. Stir gently and serve warm with more honey, maple syrup, or cream drizzled on top.

APPLE-NUT OATMEAL

SERVES: 8 • PREP TIME: 15 MINUTES • COOK TIME: 7 TO 8 HOURS ON LOW

Steel-cut oats are the only type of oats that cook well in the slow cooker. All other varieties, including regular rolled oats, get too soft when cooked for a long period of time. Steel-cut oats are made from the whole oat, cut into pieces—and are a great source of protein, fiber, and iron.

1. In a 4- or 5-quart slow cooker, stir well to combine the oats, chia seeds, apples, almond milk, apple juice, honey, brown sugar, cinnamon, nutmeg, cardamom, and salt.

2. Cover and cook on low for 7 to 8 hours, or until the oats are tender.

3. Stir gently and serve.

2 cups steel-cut oats

1 cup chia seeds

3 Granny Smith apples, peeled, cored, and chopped

6 cups almond or coconut milk

2 cups apple juice

¼ cup honey

2 tablespoons brown sugar

1 teaspoon ground cinnamon

¼ teaspoon ground nutmeg

¼ teaspoon ground cardamom

¼ teaspoon salt

The Next Day

Leftover cooked oatmeal makes a fabulous breakfast of crisp baked oatmeal. Combine 3 cups of the leftover oatmeal with 2 eggs, 1 teaspoon baking powder, ⅓ cup milk or apple juice, 2 teaspoons vanilla, and 3 tablespoons melted coconut oil. Bake at 375°F in a 9-by-13-inch pan for 40 to 50 minutes.

CHEESY SPINACH STRATA

SERVES: 6 TO 8 • PREP TIME: 25 MINUTES
COOK TIME: 7 TO 8 HOURS ON LOW, PLUS 2 TO 4 MINUTES IN THE MICROWAVE

A strata is a combination of bread, eggs, milk, cheese, and vegetables that bakes into a delicious and filling casserole. This warm and hearty recipe is great for breakfast, especially on a cold winter morning.

1. In a medium microwave-safe bowl, mix to combine the butter, onion, and leek. Partially cover and cook on high for 2 to 4 minutes, or until the vegetables are tender, stirring halfway through the cooking time.

2. In a 4- or 5-quart slow cooker, layer the bread cubes, frozen spinach, Havarti and Cheddar cheeses, and the onion mixture.

3. In a large bowl, beat well to combine the eggs, cream, Veggie Broth, marjoram, salt, and pepper. Pour the egg mixture into the slow cooker.

4. Cover and cook on low for 7 to 8 hours, or until the strata is set and a food thermometer registers 160°F.

5. Uncover, let stand for 10 minutes, and serve.

1 tablespoon butter

1 onion, chopped

1 leek, chopped

8 slices firm whole-wheat bread, cut into cubes

2 (10-ounce) packages frozen chopped spinach, thawed and well drained

2 cups shredded Havarti cheese

1 cup shredded Cheddar cheese

6 eggs

1 cup light cream

1 cup Veggie Broth (page 60)

1 teaspoon dried marjoram leaves

1 teaspoon salt

⅛ teaspoon freshly ground black pepper

Prep It Right Frozen spinach is full of water. For this recipe to succeed, you'll need to remove as much water from the thawed spinach as possible. Put the spinach in a colander, and once it is thawed, press down on it with your hands. Then put the spinach between paper towels and press to remove as much water as you can.

APPLE-PEAR STRATA

SERVES: 6 • PREP TIME: 25 MINUTES • COOK TIME: 7 TO 8 HOURS ON LOW

Stratas don't have to be savory. This sweet strata, full of delicious fruit, is a wonderful change of pace. Other fruits are great in this strata, too—peaches or nectarines, for example—in place of the pears.

1. In a large bowl, toss the apples, pears, and raisins with the lemon juice to coat.

2. In a 4- or 5-quart slow cooker, layer the apple mixture and bread cubes.

3. In another large bowl, beat well to combine the eggs, apple juice, cream, honey, cinnamon, cardamom, and salt. Pour the egg mixture into the slow cooker.

4. Cover and cook on low for 7 to 8 hours, or until the strata registers 160°F on a food thermometer.

5. Uncover, let stand for 10 minutes, and serve.

Prep It Right

All recipes containing eggs should be cooked to 160°F for food safety reasons.

- 3 Granny Smith apples, peeled, cored, and chopped
- 3 Bosc pears, peeled, cored, and chopped
- ½ cup golden raisins
- 2 tablespoons freshly squeezed lemon juice
- 8 cups firm sourdough bread, cut into cubes
- 7 eggs
- 2 cups apple juice or pear nectar
- ½ cup heavy (whipping) cream
- ¼ cup honey
- 1 teaspoon ground cinnamon
- ⅛ teaspoon ground cardamom
- ¼ teaspoon salt

BROWN SUGAR-APRICOT OATMEAL

SERVES: 6 • PREP TIME: 15 MINUTES • COOK TIME: 7 TO 8 HOURS ON LOW

Oatmeal can be flavored with so many different ingredients. Don't limit yourself to plain oatmeal served with cream and maple syrup! Two kinds of apricots add great flavor and texture to this recipe. But really, the sky's the limit.

2 cups steel-cut oats

5 dried apricots, chopped

4 fresh apricots, peeled and chopped

6 cups almond or coconut milk

2 cups apple juice

⅓ cup packed brown sugar

1 teaspoon ground cinnamon

¼ teaspoon ground nutmeg

¼ teaspoon ground ginger

¼ teaspoon salt

1. In a 4- or 5-quart slow cooker, stir well to combine the oats, dried apricots, fresh apricots, almond milk, apple juice, brown sugar, cinnamon, nutmeg, ginger, and salt.

2. Cover and cook on low for 7 to 8 hours, or until the oats are tender.

3. Stir gently and serve.

EGG *and* SWEET POTATO FRITTATA

SERVES: 8 TO 10 • PREP TIME: 25 MINUTES • COOK TIME: 7 TO 8 HOURS ON LOW

Think of a frittata as a thicker and sturdier omelet. In this version, frozen sweet potato tater tots are layered with veggies and cooked until tender in a rich egg and cheese custard.

1. In a 4- or 5-quart slow cooker, break up the thawed and drained sweet potato tater tots slightly with a large fork.

2. Add the cheese, onion, garlic, red bell peppers, and frozen sausage crumbles to the slow cooker, and stir gently.

3. In a large bowl, beat well to combine the eggs, milk, Veggie Broth, thyme, salt, and pepper. Pour the egg mixture into the slow cooker.

4. Cover and cook on low for 7 to 8 hours, or until a food thermometer registers 160°F.

5. Carefully cut and scoop to serve.

2 (20-ounce) packages frozen sweet potato tater tots, thawed and drained

2 cups shredded Cheddar cheese

1 onion, chopped

4 garlic cloves, minced

2 red bell peppers, seeded and chopped

1 (12-ounce) package frozen soy sausage crumbles, thawed

9 eggs

1 cup milk

1 cup Veggie Broth (page 60)

1 teaspoon dried thyme leaves

½ teaspoon salt

⅛ teaspoon freshly ground black pepper

DENVER STRATA

SERVES: 6 TO 8 • PREP TIME: 20 MINUTES • COOK TIME: 7 TO 8 HOURS ON LOW

A Denver omelet is made with ham or bacon, bell peppers, onion, and cheese. We'll turn that recipe into a slow cooker strata using mushrooms instead of ham, and whole-wheat English muffins. This is a great weekend brunch. Let it cook overnight, and wake up to a delicious meal.

1 cup cremini mushrooms

1 onion, chopped

1 red bell pepper, seeded and chopped

1 yellow bell pepper, seeded and chopped

8 whole-wheat English muffins, split, toasted, and cubed

2 cups shredded provolone cheese

1 cup shredded Cheddar cheese

8 eggs

1 cup light cream

3 tablespoons Dijon mustard

1 teaspoon salt

1 teaspoon dried oregano leaves

⅛ teaspoon freshly ground black pepper

½ cup grated Parmesan cheese

1. In a 4- or 5-quart slow cooker, layer the mushrooms, onion, red and yellow bell peppers, cubed English muffins, and provolone and Cheddar cheeses.

2. In a large bowl, beat the eggs, cream, mustard, salt, oregano, and pepper until well mixed and smooth.

3. Pour the egg mixture into the slow cooker, and top with the Parmesan cheese.

4. Cover and cook on low for 7 to 8 hours, or until a food thermometer registers 160°F.

5. Uncover, let stand for 10 minutes, and serve.

NUTTY GRANOLA

SERVES: 12 TO 14 • PREP TIME: 20 MINUTES • COOK TIME: 4 TO 5 HOURS ON LOW

Granola is very easy to make in the slow cooker. Once it cools, this granola keeps well, stored at room temperature in an airtight container, for about a week—if it lasts that long! Use it in other recipes, as a snack, or for an on-the-go breakfast.

9 cups old-fashioned oats

1 cup slivered almonds

1 cup chopped cashews

1 cup chopped pecans

1 cup maple syrup

½ cup melted almond butter

3 tablespoons melted coconut oil

2 teaspoons ground cinnamon

1 teaspoon salt

½ teaspoon ground nutmeg

¼ teaspoon ground cardamom

2 tablespoons vanilla

1½ cups dried cherries

1. In a 4- or 5-quart slow cooker, stir well to combine the oats, almonds, cashews, pecans, maple syrup, almond butter, coconut oil, cinnamon, salt, nutmeg, cardamom, and vanilla.

2. Cover and cook on low for 4 to 5 hours, or until fragrant and the oats are darker brown. If you are at home while the recipe cooks, stir every hour or so.

3. Stir the granola well, and then spread it over two large baking sheets. Sprinkle it with the dried cherries and let cool completely before storing in an airtight container.

Perfect Pair

Serve this granola with some almond or coconut milk poured over it. You can drizzle it with maple syrup, agave, or any other type of syrup if you'd like.

SALTED CARAMEL FRENCH TOAST

SERVES: 8 • PREP TIME: 20 MINUTES • COOK TIME: 6 TO 7 HOURS ON LOW, PLUS 15 TO 20 MINUTES IN THE OVEN

French toast made as a casserole is wonderfully creamy, with lots of delicious browned edges. Salted Almond-Caramel Sauce makes it very decadent and rich. This recipe should be made on a special occasion when you have lots of hungry guests.

1. Preheat the oven to 350°F.

2. On 2 baking sheets, bake the bread for 15 to 20 minutes, or until browned and crisp.

3. In a 5-quart slow cooker, layer the bread, and drizzle it with ⅓ cup of Almond-Caramel Sauce. Top this with the pecans, another ⅓ cup of Almond-Caramel Sauce, and the caramel bits, followed by another ⅓ cup of Almond-Caramel Sauce.

4. In a large bowl, beat the eggs with the light cream, heavy cream, brown sugar, and vanilla until smooth and well mixed. Pour the egg mixture into the slow cooker.

5. Cover and cook on low for 6 to 7 hours, or until a food thermometer registers 160°F.

6. Scoop out of the slow cooker, and serve with the remaining ½ cup of caramel sauce.

10 cups cubed ciabatta bread

1½ cups Salted Almond-Caramel Sauce (page 75), divided

2 cups small, whole pecans

1 cup caramel bits or chopped unwrapped caramels

10 eggs

1 cup light cream

1 cup heavy (whipping) cream

½ cup brown sugar

1 tablespoon vanilla

 Ciabatta bread has large holes and a crisp and chewy crust. It will soak up and hold the egg mixture and the Almond-Caramel Sauce and won't get too soggy in the slow cooker. You can substitute any other type of chewy firm bread of your choice.

CRANBERRY-MAPLE POLENTA

SERVES: 8 • PREP TIME: 15 MINUTES • COOK TIME: 6 TO 7 HOURS ON LOW

Polenta is more coarsely ground than the typical corn-meal available for purchase. It can be flavored many different ways. It's delicious served hot with some cool milk poured over the top. Polenta itself is very mild, so add lots of flavorful ingredients for more interest.

- 2½ cups medium-ground cornmeal or polenta
- 1 cup dried cranberries
- 2 cups almond milk, plus more for serving, if desired
- 2 cups white cranberry juice
- 4 cups water
- ½ cup maple syrup
- 3 tablespoons maple sugar or brown sugar, plus more for serving, if desired
- ¼ teaspoon salt

1. In a 4-quart slow cooker, stir well to combine the polenta, cranberries, almond milk, cranberry juice, water, maple syrup, maple sugar, and salt.

2. Cover and cook on low for 6 to 7 hours, or until the polenta is thick.

3. Remove the cover and stir briskly until the polenta is creamy.

4. Serve topped with more maple syrup and almond milk, if desired.

Ingredient Tip

Don't try to make polenta with finely ground cornmeal, or it will be way too soft and mushy. The best polenta (the grain itself) is made from flint corn, which has a very hard coating.

ARTICHOKE FRITTATA

SERVES: 6 • PREP TIME: 25 MINUTES • COOK TIME: 4 TO 5 HOURS ON LOW OR 2 HOURS ON HIGH

Artichokes are delicious in a frittata. This sturdy recipe is perfect for breakfast or brunch. It can be served hot or warm, or out of the refrigerator with about 20 minutes standing time. It's wonderfully versatile, which makes it great for a busy family with lots of different schedules.

1. Cut each artichoke heart into 4 pieces. Make sure they are well drained.

2. In a 4- or 5-quart slow cooker, stir gently to combine the artichoke pieces, bell peppers, onion, eggs, cream, Monterey Jack and Colby cheeses, marjoram, thyme, salt, and pepper.

3. Sprinkle with the Parmesan cheese.

4. Cover and cook on low for 4 to 5 hours, or on high for 2 hours, until the eggs are set and a food thermometer registers 160°F.

5. Carefully cut and scoop to serve.

- 2 (14-ounce) cans artichoke hearts, drained
- 2 red bell peppers, seeded and chopped
- 1 red onion, chopped
- 9 eggs
- ½ cup heavy (whipping) cream
- 2 cups shredded Monterey Jack cheese
- 1 cup shredded Colby cheese
- 1 teaspoon dried marjoram leaves
- 1 teaspoon dried thyme leaves
- 1 teaspoon salt
- ⅛ teaspoon freshly ground black pepper
- ⅓ cup Parmesan cheese

Perfect Pair This frittata is delicious served with a fresh fruit salad drizzled with a dressing made from honey and orange juice. Top with some fresh mint leaves and orange zest.

ITALIAN STRATA

SERVES: 6 TO 8 • PREP TIME: 20 MINUTES • COOK TIME: 7 TO 8 HOURS ON LOW

Classic Italian flavors include tomatoes, onions, garlic, basil, oregano, mozzarella, and Parmesan cheese. All of these ingredients combine in this hearty strata that is perfect for a holiday brunch. What better way is there to wow your guests?

1. In a 4- or 5-quart slow cooker, layer the bread, onion, garlic, tomatoes, mozzarella cheese, Asiago cheese, and provolone cheese.

2. In a large bowl, beat well to combine the eggs, Veggie Broth, milk, cream, oregano, basil, salt, and pepper until smooth. Pour the egg mixture into the slow cooker, and top with the Parmesan cheese.

3. Cover and cook on low for 7 to 8 hours, or until a food thermometer registers 160°F.

4. Uncover and let stand for 10 minutes.

5. Carefully cut and scoop to serve.

10 cups cubed
ciabatta bread

1 onion, chopped

4 garlic cloves, minced

½ cup chopped sun-dried
tomatoes in oil

1 cup shredded
mozzarella cheese

1 cup shredded
Asiago cheese

1 cup shredded
provolone cheese

9 eggs

1 cup Veggie Broth
(page 60)

2 cups milk

1 cup heavy
(whipping) cream

1 teaspoon dried
oregano leaves

1 teaspoon dried basil leaves

1 teaspoon salt

¼ teaspoon freshly ground
black pepper

½ cup grated
Parmesan cheese

TEX-MEX POTATO STRATA

SERVES: 8 • PREP TIME: 20 MINUTES • COOK TIME: 7 TO 9 HOURS ON LOW

Potatoes are wonderful in this dish, cooked until tender with lots of spicy flavors and creamy cheese. Serve it with sour cream, some salsa, and chopped avocados. I guarantee you'll do a little salsa dance in your chair while you eat this.

1. In a 4- or 5-quart slow cooker, layer the potatoes, onion, garlic, jalapeños, chipotle chiles, red bell pepper, poblano pepper, tomatillos, and Pepper Jack cheese.

2. In a large bowl, mix well to combine the sour cream, milk, Veggie Broth, adobo sauce, chili powder, oregano, salt, and pepper.

3. Pour the sour cream mixture into the slow cooker. Use a knife if necessary to make sure that the sauce has penetrated through the vegetables. Sprinkle with the Cotija cheese.

4. Cover and cook on low for 7 to 9 hours, or until the potatoes are tender.

5. Uncover and let stand for 10 minutes.

6. Carefully cut and scoop to serve.

3 pounds russet potatoes, peeled and thinly sliced

1 onion, chopped

3 garlic cloves, minced

2 jalapeño peppers, minced

2 chipotle chiles in adobo sauce, minced

1 red bell pepper, seeded and chopped

1 poblano pepper, seeded and chopped

4 tomatillos, husks removed, rinsed, and chopped

2 cups shredded Pepper Jack cheese

1½ cups sour cream

1½ cups milk

1 cup Veggie Broth (page 60)

2 tablespoons adobo sauce

2 teaspoons chili powder

1 teaspoon dried oregano leaves

1 teaspoon salt

⅛ teaspoon freshly ground black pepper

⅓ cup grated Cotija cheese

MUSHROOM-ONION STRATA

SERVES: 6 • PREP TIME: 20 MINUTES, PLUS 30 MINUTES TO SOAK • COOK TIME: 7 TO 8 HOURS ON LOW

This strata is made from four kinds of mushrooms, some of which are only available dried. Look for them in large grocery stores or specialty stores or order them online. Dried mushroom are almost always soaked first before they are added to any recipe.

1. In a medium bowl, cover the dried morel and porcini mushrooms with the hot water. Cover and let stand for 30 minutes.

2. Drain the mushrooms, reserving the soaking liquid. Strain the soaking liquid through cheesecloth to remove any grit. Reserve 1 cup of the soaking liquid.

3. Remove and discard the stems from the mushrooms if they are tough. Coarsely chop the mushrooms.

4. In a 4- or 5-quart slow cooker, layer the soaked mushrooms and button and cremini mushrooms with the bread, Caramelized Onions, and cheese.

5. In a large bowl, beat well to combine the eggs, milk, cream, reserved mushroom soaking liquid, marjoram, salt, and pepper until smooth. Pour the egg mixture into the slow cooker.

6. Cover and cook on low for 7 to 8 hours, or until a food thermometer registers 160°F.

7. Uncover and let stand for 10 minutes.

8. Carefully cut and scoop to serve.

1 ounce dried morel mushrooms

1 cup hot water

1 cup sliced button mushrooms

1 cup sliced cremini mushrooms

11 cups cubed whole-wheat bread, toasted

1 cup Caramelized Onions (page 181)

2 cups shredded Taleggio or Gouda cheese

8 eggs

1 cup milk

1 cup heavy (whipping) cream

1 teaspoon dried marjoram leaves

1 teaspoon salt

⅛ teaspoon freshly ground black pepper

DIPS & SNACKS

CHAPTER TEN

CHEESY SPINACH DIP

SERVES: 8 • PREP TIME: 20 MINUTES • COOK TIME: 4 TO 6 HOURS ON LOW

Both frozen and fresh spinach are used in this dip recipe, adding lots of fresh flavor and color. Serve this dip with crackers, tortilla chips, sturdy potato chips, and lots of crudités for a great appetizer. Needless to say, it's a hit at parties.

1. In a 3-quart slow cooker, stir well to combine the onion, garlic, red bell pepper, frozen spinach, cream cheese, Swiss, Monterey Jack, provolone, and Parmesan cheese, thyme, salt, pepper, and fresh spinach.

2. Cover and cook on low for 4 to 6 hours, or until the dip is bubbly and browned around the edges.

3. Stir gently and serve.

1 onion, chopped

3 garlic cloves, sliced

1 red bell pepper, seeded and chopped

1 (10-ounce) package frozen chopped spinach, thawed and drained

1 (8-ounce) package cream cheese, cut into cubes

1 cup shredded Swiss cheese

1 cup shredded Monterey Jack cheese

1 cup shredded provolone cheese

½ cup grated Parmesan cheese

1 teaspoon dried thyme leaves

½ teaspoon salt

⅛ teaspoon freshly ground black pepper

2 cups fresh baby spinach leaves

CREAMY ARTICHOKE DIP

SERVES: 8 • PREP TIME: 15 MINUTES • COOK TIME: 4 TO 6 HOURS ON LOW

This dip is typically loaded with a lot of salt and fat. I prefer making this recipe with a lot more vegetables to make the dip more colorful and healthier. And tastier!

1. Put the soft tofu on a plate, and let it stand for 10 minutes to drain while you get the other ingredients ready.

2. In a 4-quart slow cooker, stir well to combine the artichoke hearts, red onion, red bell peppers, garlic, cream cheese, almond milk, dill, salt, and pepper. Pour the liquid off the soft tofu, and add the tofu to the slow cooker; stir gently.

3. Cover and cook on low for 4 to 6 hours, or until the dip is hot and bubbly.

4. Stir gently and serve.

- 1 (12-ounce) package soft tofu
- 2 (14-ounce) cans artichoke hearts, drained and coarsely chopped
- 1 red onion, chopped
- 2 red bell peppers, seeded and chopped
- 5 garlic cloves, minced
- 1 (8-ounce) package vegan cream cheese, cubed
- ¼ cup almond milk
- 3 tablespoons minced fresh dill
- ½ teaspoon salt
- ⅛ teaspoon freshly ground black pepper

Perfect Pair

This dip is wonderful with toasted garlic bread. Slice French bread very thin and drizzle with olive oil. Toast the bread in a 400°F oven, and then rub each slice with a cut garlic clove.

MARINATED MUSHROOMS

SERVES: 8 • PREP TIME: 25 MINUTES • COOK TIME: 6 TO 8 HOURS ON LOW

Mushrooms make a wonderful appetizer. The sauce in this recipe is really good. You may want to serve the mushrooms with tiny plates and forks, but they can be served with appetizer picks, too.

1. In a 4-quart slow cooker, stir gently to combine the button, cremini, and shiitake mushrooms, onion, garlic, olive oil, lemon juice, dill seed, salt, marjoram, and pepper.

2. Cover and cook on low for 6 to 8 hours, or until the mushrooms are very tender, and serve.

To prepare mushrooms, rinse them under cold running water very briefly or wipe with a damp towel. Cut off the end of the stems, and then cut the mushrooms into ½-inch thick slices. Never soak fresh mushrooms in water—they will absorb it and the dish will be watery.

1 (8-ounce) package button mushrooms, sliced

1 (8-ounce) package cremini mushrooms, sliced

1 (8-ounce) package shiitake mushrooms, sliced

1 onion, chopped

3 garlic cloves, minced

¼ cup extra-virgin olive oil

2 tablespoons freshly squeezed lemon juice

½ teaspoon dill seed

1 teaspoon salt

1 teaspoon dried marjoram leaves

⅛ teaspoon freshly ground black pepper

CHEESY CARAMELIZED ONION DIP

SERVES: 8 TO 10 • PREP TIME: 25 MINUTES • COOK TIME: 9 TO 12 HOURS ON LOW

This dip takes the ubiquitous packaged onion dip to the next level. There's nothing as good as caramelized onions enveloped in a creamy and cheesy, thick and rich sauce. Serve this at a party, and everyone will cluster around the bowl. Trust me, it goes fast.

1. In a 3-quart slow cooker, stir well to combine the chopped and sliced onions, garlic, olive oil, salt, and pepper.

2. Cover and cook on low for 8 to 10 hours, or until the onions are deep golden brown. If you are at home during cooking time, stir the onions once or twice.

3. Stir in the thyme, cream cheese, sour cream, Swiss cheese, provolone cheese, and Parmesan cheese.

4. Cover and cook on low for another 1 to 2 hours, or until the dip is creamy and smooth.

5. Stir gently and serve.

- 2 onions, chopped
- 2 onions, sliced
- 5 garlic cloves, sliced
- 2 tablespoons olive oil
- ½ teaspoon salt
- ⅛ teaspoon freshly ground black pepper
- 1 teaspoon dried thyme leaves
- 2 (8-ounce) packages cream cheese, cubed
- ½ cup sour cream
- 1 cup shredded Swiss cheese
- 1 cup shredded provolone cheese
- ½ cup grated Parmesan cheese

Substitute Tip

If you want to make this dip vegan, add 2 packages of vegan cream cheese and 1 (12-ounce) package silken tofu in place of the cream cheese and Swiss, provolone, and Parmesan cheeses.

GIGANTE BEAN SALAD
with ONION *and* PARSLEY

SERVES: 8 • PREP TIME: 15 MINUTES, PLUS OVERNIGHT TO SOAK • COOK TIME: 8 TO 10 HOURS ON LOW

Gigante beans are very large white beans from Greece. They can be found online or at specialty international markets. If you can't find them, substitute dried Great Northern or cannellini beans in this refreshing salad recipe.

1. Sort the beans, rinse well, and drain. In a 4- or 5-quart slow cooker, cover with cool water. Let stand overnight.

2. In the morning, drain the beans, discarding the soaking liquid. In the slow cooker, stir well to combine the beans, Veggie Broth, yellow onion, garlic, salt, and pepper.

3. Cover and cook on low for 8 to 10 hours, or until the beans are tender. Drain if necessary.

4. In a large bowl, whisk well to combine the olive oil, vinegar, and mustard. Season to taste with salt and pepper.

5. Add the cooked and drained bean mixture, red onion, and parsley to the bowl with the dressing, and stir to combine. Serve immediately, or cover and chill for 3 to 4 hours before serving.

1 pound dried Gigante beans

5 cups Veggie Broth
(page 60)

1 yellow or white onion,
chopped

5 garlic cloves, minced

1 teaspoon salt

⅛ teaspoon freshly ground
black pepper

⅔ cup extra-virgin olive oil

⅓ cup white balsamic
vinegar

2 tablespoons Dijon mustard

1 sweet red onion, chopped

1 cup chopped fresh flat-leaf
parsley

FRUIT *and* NUT MIX

SERVES: 12 TO 14 • PREP TIME: 20 MINUTES • COOK TIME: 5 TO 6 HOURS ON LOW

Any snack mix makes a welcome gift, or a great treat during a hike or any outdoor event. This mix is flavored with lots of spices and has soft dried fruit added to it. Pack it in small plastic bags and tuck it into your backpack.

2 cups rice squares cereal

2 cups oat squares cereal

2 cups whole small pecans

2 cups macadamia nuts or slivered almonds

2 cups cashews

¼ cup olive oil

1 teaspoon seasoned salt

1 teaspoon dried marjoram leaves

1 teaspoon dried thyme leaves

2 cups dried cherries

1 cup golden raisins

1 cup dried currants

1. In a 4- or 5-quart slow cooker, combine the rice squares, oat squares, pecans, macadamias, and cashews.

2. Drizzle the nuts with the olive oil, and sprinkle with the salt, marjoram, and thyme. Stir gently.

3. Cover and cook on low for 5 to 6 hours, or until the nuts are toasted. If you are at home while this is cooking, stir the mixture every hour or so.

4. Transfer the mixture to a large bowl, and stir in the cherries, raisins, and currants.

5. On 2 large baking sheets, spread the mixture out and let it cool.

6. Store in airtight containers at room temperature for up to 2 weeks.

Substitute Tip

You can use any cereal you'd like and any type of nuts in this easy recipe. You can even vary the proportions. When you hit upon a combination that you like, write it down so you can make it over and over again.

HERB-ROASTED NUT MIX

SERVES: 10 TO 12 • PREP TIME: 15 MINUTES • COOK TIME: 2 TO 3 HOURS ON LOW

If you love nuts, this is the slow cooker recipe for you. The slow cooker roasts nuts to perfection with no attention from you. Both dried and fresh herbs add to the depth of flavor. It's a great afternoon snack when you need an extra boost to get through the rest of the day.

2 cups small whole pecans

2 cups whole almonds

2 cups walnuts

2 cups cashews

1 tablespoon coconut oil

2 teaspoons dried thyme leaves

1 teaspoon dried basil leaves

1 teaspoon dried marjoram leaves

1½ teaspoons salt

1 tablespoon minced fresh thyme leaves

1. In a 4- or 5-quart slow cooker, stir gently to combine the pecans, almonds, walnuts, cashews, coconut oil, dried thyme, basil, marjoram, and salt.

2. Cover and cook on low for 2 to 3 hours, stirring every hour so the nuts don't burn.

3. Uncover and stir in the fresh thyme.

4. Spread the nuts on 2 baking sheets and let cool, stirring occasionally.

5. Store in an airtight container at room temperature for up to 1 week.

Substitute Tip
You can make this recipe with many different kinds of nuts, or use just one kind. Other good choices include hazelnuts, macadamia nuts, peanuts, and pistachios.

GLAZED ALMONDS

SERVES: 10 TO 12 • PREP TIME: 15 MINUTES • COOK TIME: 3 TO 4 HOURS ON LOW

Whole almonds can be purchased with the skin on or off. If you can find them, Marcona almonds from Spain are fabulous in this recipe. Those almonds have a creamy texture and buttery taste. These are a great party favor at the holidays, too.

1. In a 4-quart slow cooker, stir gently to combine the almonds, golden syrup, maple syrup, agave nectar, brown sugar, vanilla, and almond butter.

2. Cover and cook on low for 3 to 4 hours, stirring every hour, or until the nuts are toasted.

3. Remove the nuts from the slow cooker and spread on a baking sheet. Sprinkle with the salt and cayenne pepper, and let cool completely.

4. Store in an airtight container at room temperature for up to 1 week.

6 cups skinned almonds or Marcona almonds

3 tablespoons Lyle's Golden Syrup

3 tablespoons maple syrup

1 tablespoon agave nectar

2 tablespoons brown sugar

1 tablespoon vanilla

2 tablespoons almond butter

1½ teaspoons salt

⅛ teaspoon ground cayenne pepper

Ingredient Tip

Lyle's Golden Syrup is an English pantry staple. It is a thick, golden type of inverted sugar syrup. You can find it at most large grocery stores and online. If you can't find it, use more maple syrup and agave nectar.

ROASTED TOMATO DIP

SERVES: 8 TO 10 • PREP TIME: 20 MINUTES • COOK TIME: 8 TO 10 HOURS ON LOW

Roasting tomatoes concentrates their flavors and makes this vegetable taste sweet and rich. Here, adding just a few more ingredients transforms this kitchen staple into a delicious and healthy dip.

16 Roma tomatoes, halved

6 beefsteak tomatoes, sliced

1 (8-ounce) container cherry tomatoes, halved

6 sun-dried tomatoes in oil, chopped

1 red onion, chopped

4 garlic cloves, sliced

5 tablespoons olive oil

1 teaspoon honey

1 teaspoon salt

1 teaspoon dried marjoram leaves

⅛ teaspoon freshly ground black pepper

1. In a 4- or 5-quart slow cooker, stir well to combine the Roma tomatoes, beefsteak tomatoes, cherry tomatoes, sun-dried tomatoes, red onion, garlic, olive oil, honey, salt, marjoram, and pepper.

2. Leave the cover off the slow cooker, and cook on low for 8 to 10 hours, or until the tomatoes look thick and start to brown around the edges.

3. You can leave the texture as is at this point, or mash or purée the tomato mixture right in the slow cooker for a smoother version.

4. Store in an airtight container at room temperature for up to 1 week.

The Next Day Use this fabulous mixture in any pasta sauce or as a spread on toast for Bruschetta. It's delicious added to any soup or stew that uses tomatoes, too.

MUSHROOMS *for* CROSTINI

SERVES: 8 TO 10 • PREP TIME: 20 MINUTES, PLUS 20 MINUTES TO SOAK
COOK TIME: 7 TO 9 HOURS ON LOW

Crostini is simply toasted bread topped with cheeses, beans, or vegetables or a combination of all three. You can use regular gluten-free bread as the base for this mushroom mixture, or use it as a topping on zucchini or yellow summer squash slices.

1 ounce dried morel mushrooms

1 cup hot water

1 (8-ounce) package button mushrooms, sliced

1 (8-ounce) package cremini mushrooms, sliced

2 onions, chopped

5 garlic cloves, minced

2 tablespoons olive oil

1 teaspoon salt

1 teaspoon dried marjoram leaves

2 fresh thyme sprigs

1/8 teaspoon freshly ground black pepper

1/8 teaspoon ground cayenne pepper

1. In a small bowl, cover the morel mushrooms with the hot water. Let stand for 20 minutes.

2. Drain the mushrooms, reserving the soaking liquid. Strain the soaking liquid through cheesecloth to remove any grit. Remove and discard the mushroom stems if they are tough, and slice the mushrooms.

3. In a 4-quart slow cooker, stir well to combine the morel mushrooms and 1/4 cup of the mushroom soaking liquid with the button and cremini mushrooms, onions, garlic, olive oil, salt, marjoram, thyme, black pepper, and cayenne pepper.

4. Cover and cook on low for 7 to 9 hours, or until the mushrooms are tender.

5. Remove and discard the thyme stems.

6. If you'd like to thicken the mixture, uncover and cook on high for 1 hour longer, stirring occasionally.

EGGPLANT TAPENADE

SERVES: 8 TO 10 • PREP TIME: 25 MINUTES • COOK TIME: 7 TO 9 HOURS ON LOW

Tapenade originated in the Provence region of France and is traditionally made from olives, capers, olive oil, and usually anchovies. It has evolved to include any number and combination of flavors; I like eggplant and mushrooms in place of the anchovies for great depth of flavor. Serve this recipe as a dip or as a topping for toasted bread.

1. In a 4- or 5-quart slow cooker, stir well to combine the eggplant, tomatoes, onions, garlic, green olives, Kalamata olives, capers, lemon juice, thyme, black pepper, and cayenne pepper.

2. Cover and cook on low for 7 to 9 hours, or until the mixture is blended.

3. Remove and discard the thyme stems.

4. You can leave the vegetables as they are, or mash or purée them for a different consistency. Serve hot, cold, or at room temperature.

1 large eggplant, peeled and chopped

3 beefsteak tomatoes, seeded and chopped

2 onions, chopped

6 garlic cloves, sliced

½ cup chopped green olives

½ cup chopped Kalamata olives

2 tablespoons capers, rinsed and drained

2 tablespoons freshly squeezed lemon juice

2 fresh thyme sprigs

⅛ teaspoon freshly ground black pepper

⅛ teaspoon ground cayenne pepper

CAPONATA

SERVES: 8 • PREP TIME: 25 MINUTES • COOK TIME: 6 TO 8 HOURS ON LOW

Caponata's original home is Sicily, where the dish is made from eggplant and other vegetables. It can be served as a salad or as an appetizer dip or spread. However you enjoy it, sip some wine, close your eyes, and imagine you're enjoying the warm breeze.

1. In a 4- or 5-quart slow cooker, stir well to combine the eggplant, tomatoes, onion, celery, red and yellow bell peppers, garlic, raisins, tomato paste, honey, lemon juice, basil, oregano, salt, and pepper.

2. Cover and cook on low for 6 to 8 hours, or until the vegetables are tender and a sauce has formed.

3. Stir gently and serve.

The Next Day Caponata makes a wonderful sandwich spread, or a delicious topping for grilled tofu. Add it to soups or stews or to salad dressings for a nice change of pace. It freezes well, too, for later use.

1 large eggplant, peeled and cubed

3 beefsteak tomatoes, seeded and chopped

2 onions, chopped

6 celery stalks, sliced

2 red bell peppers, seeded and chopped

1 yellow bell pepper, seeded and chopped

6 garlic cloves, sliced

½ cup golden raisins

¼ cup tomato paste

2 tablespoons honey

2 tablespoons freshly squeezed lemon juice

1 teaspoon dried basil leaves

1 teaspoon dried oregano leaves

1 teaspoon salt

⅛ teaspoon freshly ground black pepper

PEPPERY REFRIED BEAN DIP

SERVES: 8 • PREP TIME: 15 MINUTES • COOK TIME: 6 TO 8 HOURS ON LOW

I love refried beans and put them into just about any main dish. This spicy dip is a perfect appetizer before a dinner of enchiladas or burritos. Garnishing the dip with a bit of cilantro and chopped tomatoes adds a nice finishing touch and a cheery pop of color.

1. In a 4-quart slow cooker, stir well to combine the refried beans, kidney beans, onions, garlic, jalapeños, red bell peppers, chipotle chiles, adobo sauce, chili powder, cumin seeds, salt, and cayenne pepper.

2. Cover and cook on low for 6 to 8 hours, or until the dip is hot.

3. Stir gently, top with the grape tomatoes and cilantro, and serve.

Prep It Right

You can serve hot dips right in the slow cooker (if it's nice looking). Otherwise, transfer the hot dip to a fondue pot or heated serving dish placed over a candle or Sterno to keep it warm while serving.

2 (15-ounce) cans vegetarian refried beans (make sure it's vegan if needed)

1 (15-ounce) can kidney beans, rinsed and drained

2 onions, chopped

5 garlic cloves, minced

2 jalapeño or habanero peppers, minced

2 red bell peppers, seeded and chopped

2 chipotle chiles in adobo sauce, minced

2 tablespoons adobo sauce

1 tablespoon chili powder

1 teaspoon cumin seeds

1 teaspoon salt

1/8 teaspoon ground cayenne pepper

1 cup chopped grape tomatoes

1/3 cup chopped fresh cilantro

POTATOES SATAY

SERVES: 8 TO 10 • PREP TIME: 15 MINUTES • COOK TIME: 6 TO 8 HOURS ON LOW

Satay brings the flavors of Indonesia to your home. It is made from peanut butter, lemongrass, lots of spices, and soy sauce. I love serving the sauce with tiny little tender potatoes. Serve on a plate with a small fork.

1. Rinse the potatoes, and scrub them gently. Be careful, because the skins are tender.

2. In a 4-quart slow cooker, stir gently to combine the potatoes with the onion, garlic, lemongrass, Veggie Broth, peanut butter, lime juice, honey, chipotle chiles, salt, and red pepper flakes.

3. Cover and cook on low for 6 to 8 hours, or until the potatoes are tender.

4. Remove and discard the lemongrass, stir gently to mix the potatoes into the sauce, and serve.

3 pounds creamer potatoes

1 onion, finely chopped

5 garlic cloves, minced

1 lemongrass stalk, bent

⅓ cup Veggie Broth (page 60)

1 cup peanut butter

3 tablespoons freshly squeezed lime juice

1 tablespoon honey

2 chipotle chiles, minced

1 teaspoon salt

⅛ teaspoon crushed red pepper flakes

RED LENTIL–EGGPLANT DIP

SERVES: 8 TO 10 • PREP TIME: 15 MINUTES • COOK TIME: 7 TO 10 HOURS ON LOW

Lentils, those little gems that are so good in soups and stews, also make a delicious dip. This dip has a kick, because it uses sambal oelek, an Indonesian chili paste made from hot red peppers, vinegar, and salt. If you can't find it, sriracha is a good substitute.

1. Sort the lentils, rinse well, and drain.

2. In a 3- or 4-quart slow cooker, stir well to combine the lentils, eggplant, onion, garlic, Veggie Broth, honey, chile peppers, sambal oelek, oregano, salt, and pepper.

3. Cover and cook on low for 6 to 8 hours, or until the lentils and vegetables are very tender.

4. Stir in the silken tofu, cover, and cook on low for another 1 to 2 hours, or until the dip is thickened.

5. Stir in the walnuts and serve immediately, or put in a large bowl, cover, and chill for 3 to 4 hours before serving.

2 cups red lentils

1 eggplant, peeled and chopped

1 onion, chopped

8 garlic cloves, minced

4 cups Veggie Broth (page 60)

2 tablespoons honey

2 small dried red chile peppers

1 to 2 tablespoons sambal oelek

1 teaspoon dried oregano leaves

1 teaspoon salt

1/8 teaspoon freshly ground black pepper

1 cup silken tofu

1 cup chopped walnuts

BREADS

BANANA-PEAR BREAD

SERVES: 8 • PREP TIME: 15 MINUTES • COOK TIME: 3 TO 4 HOURS ON LOW

Everyone has had banana bread at one time or another, but adding some pear gives the bread a wonderful sweet and tart flavor. This bread is perfect for breakfast on a busy morning.

½ cup butter, at room temperature

⅔ cup brown sugar

⅓ cup sugar

2 eggs

2 large very ripe bananas, mashed

1 (4-ounce) jar pear baby food

2 teaspoons vanilla

1⅔ cups all-purpose flour

½ cup whole-wheat flour

1 teaspoon baking powder

¼ teaspoon salt

Nonstick baking spray with flour

1. In a large bowl, beat well to combine the butter, brown sugar, and sugar until fluffy.

2. Beat in the eggs, one at a time.

3. Stir in the mashed bananas, pear baby food, and vanilla, mixing well.

4. Add the all-purpose flour, whole-wheat flour, baking powder, and salt, and mix just until combined.

5. Spray a 9-by-5-inch loaf pan with the nonstick baking spray, and add the batter.

6. Set the pan in a 5-quart slow cooker.

7. Cover and cook on low for 3 to 4 hours, or until a toothpick inserted into the bread comes out clean.

8. Carefully remove the loaf pan from the slow cooker and let it cool for 20 minutes.

9. Remove the bread from the pan, and cool it completely on a wire rack.

Prep It Right Whenever you make bread in a slow cooker, be sure that you check the bread frequently the first time you make it. Slow cookers are all different, and some cook hotter than others. When you know how long it takes for bread to bake in your appliance, you can relax and let it do its thing.

POPPY SEED BREAD

SERVES: 8 • PREP TIME: 15 MINUTES • COOK TIME: 1½ TO 2 HOURS ON HIGH

With the new gluten-free flour mixes available—in most large grocery stores or online—anyone who must avoid this protein no longer has to mix a combination of non-wheat flours. The texture of this bread is similar to bread made with wheat flour.

1. In a large bowl, mix well to combine the gluten-free flour, millet flour, sugar, brown sugar, baking powder, baking soda, salt, and poppy seeds.

2. In a medium bowl, beat well to combine the orange juice, orange zest, butter, buttermilk, sour cream, eggs, and vanilla.

3. Stir the wet ingredients into the dry ingredients just until combined.

4. Spray a 5-quart slow cooker with the nonstick baking spray. Make an aluminum foil sling, and put it into the slow cooker; spray it with the baking spray, too. Spoon the batter into the slow cooker.

5. Cover and cook on high for 1½ to 2 hours, or until the bread springs back when lightly touched and starts to come away from the sides of the pan.

6. Remove the ceramic insert from the slow cooker, and let it stand for 20 minutes.

7. Remove the bread from the sling, and let it cool on a wire rack.

2 cups all-purpose gluten-free flour

2 tablespoons millet flour

½ cup sugar

¼ cup brown sugar

1½ teaspoons baking powder

½ teaspoon baking soda

¼ teaspoon salt

3 tablespoons poppy seeds

3 tablespoons freshly squeezed orange juice

1 teaspoon orange zest

⅓ cup butter, melted

½ cup buttermilk

½ cup sour cream

2 eggs

2 teaspoons vanilla

Nonstick baking spray with flour

HERB BREAD

SERVES: 8 • PREP TIME: 15 MINUTES, PLUS 10 MINUTES TO STAND AND 1 HOUR TO RISE
COOK TIME: 2 TO 3 HOURS ON HIGH

Making bread in the slow cooker is a great way to get fresh bread when it's too hot to turn on your oven. While many breads will rise as the slow cooker heats up, meaning there's no need for a separate rising period, this particular bread is an exception to that. Parchment paper is a necessity when you bake bread in this appliance.

1. In a large bowl, mix to combine the water, yeast, and sugar. Let stand for 10 minutes.

2. Add the bread flour, basil, thyme, marjoram, salt, and olive oil, and stir until just combined. Gradually stir in enough of the whole-wheat flour to make a soft dough. The dough should feel soft and should hold together, but should be easy to manipulate. You might not use all of the whole-wheat flour.

3. Knead the dough in the bowl for about 5 minutes. Cover the bowl with a kitchen towel, and let rise for 1 hour.

4. Tear off a long sheet of parchment paper, and put it in a 4- or 5-quart slow cooker as a liner.

1⅓ cups warm water

1 (0.25-ounce) package active dry yeast

2 teaspoons sugar

2 cups bread flour

1 teaspoon dried basil leaves

1 teaspoon dried thyme leaves

1 teaspoon dried marjoram leaves

1 teaspoon salt

¼ cup olive oil

2 cups whole-wheat flour

5. Punch down the dough, and form it into a round loaf. Place it in the center of the parchment paper in the slow cooker.

6. Turn the slow cooker to high. Layer 4 paper towels over the top of the slow cooker, making sure they are not touching the dough. Carefully place the slow cooker cover on the paper towels, trapping them between the cover and the insert. This will absorb moisture as the bread cooks.

7. Cook for 2 to 3 hours on high, or until the bread is firm. When checking, be sure to watch out for escaping steam—it can burn you.

8. Use the parchment to carefully remove the bread from the slow cooker, then discard the parchment. Set the bread to cool on a wire rack.

Breads cooked in the slow cooker will not have a brown crust because the heat isn't high enough to create non-enzymatic browning. You can briefly broil the bread when it comes out of the slow cooker for a brown and crunchy crust if you'd like.

PUMPKIN-NUT BREAD

SERVES: 8 • PREP TIME: 15 MINUTES • COOK TIME: 2 TO 3 HOURS ON HIGH

Pumpkin bread is a wonderful recipe that is perfect for breakfast on the run. And you can use it to make Pumpkin Bread Pudding (page 252), a favorite holiday treat in my house.

1. In a large bowl, beat well to combine the butter, brown sugar, and sugar. Stir in the pumpkin, and then add the eggs, egg white, and vanilla.

2. Stir in the flour mix, baking powder, baking soda, cinnamon, nutmeg, ginger, cardamom, and salt, and mix just until combined. Stir in the nuts (if using).

3. Spray a 9-by-5-inch loaf pan with the nonstick baking spray, and spoon the batter into the pan.

4. Set the pan in a 4- or 5-quart slow cooker. Add the water to the slow cooker, creating a bath around the loaf pan.

5. Cover the top of the slow cooker with a stack of 8 paper towels to absorb moisture as the bread cooks.

6. Cover and cook on high for 2 to 3 hours, or until a toothpick inserted into the bread comes out almost clean.

7. Remove the bread from the slow cooker, and let it cool for 15 minutes.

8. Remove the bread from the pan, and cool completely on a wire rack.

- ½ cup butter, at room temperature
- ¾ cup brown sugar
- 2 tablespoons sugar
- 1 (15-ounce) can solid pack pumpkin purée (not pumpkin pie filling)
- 2 eggs
- 1 egg white
- 2 teaspoons vanilla
- 1½ cups gluten-free flour mix
- 1 teaspoon baking powder
- ½ teaspoon baking soda
- 1 teaspoon ground cinnamon
- ¼ teaspoon ground nutmeg
- ¼ teaspoon ground ginger
- ⅛ teaspoon ground cardamom
- ⅛ teaspoon salt
- 1 cup chopped walnuts or pecans (optional)
- Nonstick baking spray with flour
- 1 cup water

Prep It Right

Quick breads are even better the day after they are made. Store them in an airtight container at room temperature for up to 3 days.

PINEAPPLE-CHERRY BREAD

SERVES: 8 • PREP TIME: 15 MINUTES • COOK TIME: 3 TO 4 HOURS ON LOW

Canned pineapple makes a wonderful quick bread with great flavor. The pineapple caramelizes slightly while the bread cooks, lending a tasty depth of flavor to the recipe.

- ⅓ cup butter, at room temperature
- ½ cup brown sugar
- ¼ cup sugar
- 2 eggs
- 2 teaspoons vanilla
- 1 (8-ounce) can crushed pineapple, undrained
- 1⅔ cups all-purpose flour
- 1 teaspoon baking powder
- ½ teaspoon baking soda
- ⅛ teaspoon salt
- ½ cup dried cherries
- Nonstick baking spray with flour
- 1 cup water

1. In a large bowl, beat well to combine the butter, brown sugar, and sugar. Stir in the eggs, vanilla, and undrained pineapple.

2. Mix in the flour, baking powder, baking soda, and salt until just combined, and then stir in the dried cherries.

3. Spray a 9-by-5-inch loaf pan with the nonstick baking spray, and spoon the batter into the pan.

4. Set the pan in a 4- or 5-quart slow cooker. Add the water to the slow cooker to create a bath around the loaf pan.

5. Cover the top of the slow cooker with a stack of 8 paper towels to absorb moisture as the bread cooks.

6. Cover and cook on low for 3 to 4 hours, or until a toothpick inserted into the bread comes out almost clean.

7. Remove the bread from the slow cooker, and let it cool for 15 minutes.

8. Remove the bread from the pan, and cool completely on a wire rack.

PEACH-ALMOND BREAD

SERVES: 8 • PREP TIME: 15 MINUTES • COOK TIME: 4 TO 5 HOURS ON LOW

The best use for canned peaches and pears is in baking. They make an excellent cake and a really superb quick bread. This bread is a great way to have that flavor of fresh summer peaches all year round.

1. In a large bowl, beat well to combine the butter, sugar, and brown sugar. Stir in the egg, egg white, puréed peaches, vanilla, and lemon juice.

2. Add the flour mix, ground almonds (if using), baking powder, baking soda, cinnamon, and salt, and mix just until combined. Stir in the chopped almonds (if using).

3. Spray a 9-by-5-inch loaf pan with the nonstick baking spray, and spoon the batter into the pan.

4. Set the pan in a 4- or 5-quart slow cooker. Add the water to the slow cooker to create a bath around the loaf pan.

5. Cover the top of the slow cooker with a stack of 8 paper towels to absorb moisture as the bread cooks.

6. Cover and cook on low for 4 to 5 hours, or until a toothpick inserted into the bread comes out almost clean.

7. Carefully remove the loaf pan from the slow cooker and let cool for 15 minutes.

8. Remove the bread from the pan and cool completely on a wire rack.

⅓ cup butter, at room temperature

½ cup sugar

2 tablespoons brown sugar

1 egg

1 egg white

1 (8-ounce) can peaches, undrained, puréed

2 teaspoons vanilla

1 tablespoon freshly squeezed lemon juice

1¾ cups gluten-free flour mix

¼ cup ground almonds (optional)

1 teaspoon baking powder

½ teaspoon baking soda

½ teaspoon ground cinnamon

¼ teaspoon salt

⅓ cup chopped almonds (optional)

Nonstick baking spray with flour

1 cup water

PUMPKIN SEED-BLUEBERRY BREAD

SERVES: 8 TO 10 • PREP TIME: 20 MINUTES, PLUS 1 HOUR TO RISE AND 10 MINUTES TO STAND
COOK TIME: 2 TO 3 HOURS ON HIGH

Pumpkins and dried blueberries make a great addition to a tender yeast bread. If you want this bread browned, take it out of the slow cooker when it's done and brown under the broiler, watching carefully.

1. In a large bowl, mix to combine the water, yeast, and sugar. Let stand for 10 minutes.

2. Add the bread flour, butter, and salt to the bowl, and stir until just combined. Gradually stir in enough of the all-purpose flour to make a soft dough. Stir in the pumpkin seeds and dried blueberries.

3. Knead the dough in the bowl for about 5 minutes. Cover with a kitchen towel and let rise for 1 hour.

4. Tear off a long sheet of parchment paper, and put it in the slow cooker liner.

5. Punch down the dough and form into a round loaf. Set it in the center of the parchment paper in the slow cooker.

6. Turn the slow cooker to high. Layer four paper towels on top of each other, and place them over the top of the insert so they cover the dough without touching it. Put the slow cooker cover on the paper towels, trapping them between the cover and the insert.

7. Cook for 2 to 3 hours, or until the bread is firm.

8. Remove the bread and cool it on a wire rack.

1⅓ cups warm water

1 (0.25-ounce) package active dry yeast

2 teaspoons sugar

2 cups bread flour

¼ cup butter, melted

1 teaspoon salt

2 cups all-purpose flour

⅔ cup pumpkin seeds

½ cup dried blueberries

CINNAMON-CARAMEL ROLLS

SERVES: 12 • PREP TIME: 30 MINUTES • COOK TIME: 1 HOUR ON KEEP WARM, PLUS 2 HOURS ON LOW

Yes, you can make caramel rolls in the slow cooker! The rolls are perfect for brunch on a holiday or another special occasion. The Salted Almond-Caramel Sauce recipe found in this book goes great with these, but you can use store-bought sauce to save time.

1. Spray a 5-quart slow cooker with the nonstick baking spray. Pour the Salted Almond-Caramel Sauce into the slow cooker, and set aside.

2. In a small saucepan over low heat, heat the 2 tablespoons of coconut oil and the coconut milk and honey just until warm, about 110°F. Remove the pan from the heat.

3. Sprinkle the yeast over the liquid in the saucepan, and let it stand for 5 minutes.

4. In a large bowl, combine the bread flour, all-purpose flour, ½ teaspoon of cinnamon, and salt. Add the yeast mixture, and beat until just combined.

5. Knead the dough right in the bowl, adding more all-purpose flour as needed, until it is soft and springy. Let the dough stand in the bowl while you make the filling.

Nonstick baking spray with flour

½ cup Salted Almond-Caramel Sauce (page 75) or purchased ice cream caramel sauce

2 tablespoons coconut oil, plus 1 tablespoon melted, divided

⅓ cup coconut milk

3 tablespoons honey

1 (0.25-ounce) package active dry yeast

1 cup bread flour

1 cup all-purpose flour, plus more for dusting

1½ teaspoons ground cinnamon, divided

⅛ teaspoon salt

⅓ cup brown sugar

1 tablespoon coconut oil, melted

6. For the filling, in a small bowl, mix brown sugar, 1 tablespoon of melted coconut oil, and remaining 1 teaspoon of cinnamon well.

7. On a floured surface, roll the dough into a 10-by-14-inch rectangle. Spread the brown sugar mixture over the top, and roll up the dough into a log, starting with the 14-inch side.

8. Cut the dough into 12 even rolls, and place the rolls on top of the sauce in the slow cooker.

9. Turn the slow cooker to "keep warm" for 1 hour, and then turn it to low and bake for about 2 hours, or until the caramel rolls are firm when touched with your finger.

10. Immediately invert the rolls from the slow cooker onto a wire rack and let cool for about 20 minutes before serving.

 The caramel will harden as the rolls cool. To serve them the next day, microwave one roll at a time for about 10 to 15 seconds, or until the caramel is soft again.

OAT BREAD

SERVES: 8 • PREP TIME: 15 MINUTES • COOK TIME: 2 TO 2 ½ HOURS ON HIGH

Oatmeal makes a wonderful bread with the perfect texture. This bread is great to toast. Spread it with whipped honey or cinnamon sugar for a nice treat in the morning. It's one that will get the kids out of bed and moving.

½ cup warm water

1 (0.25-ounce) package active dry yeast

½ cup apple juice

2 tablespoons melted coconut oil

2 tablespoons honey

1 cup old-fashioned oats

⅛ teaspoon salt

½ cup bread flour

½ cup whole-wheat flour

1 to 2 cups all-purpose flour

Nonstick baking spray with flour

1. In a large bowl, mix to combine the warm water with the yeast. Let stand for 5 minutes, or until bubbly.

2. Add the apple juice, coconut oil, honey, oats, and salt, and mix well.

3. Stir in the bread flour and whole-wheat flour, and beat for 1 minute. Then add enough of the all-purpose flour to make a firm dough.

4. Knead the dough right in the bowl, adding all-purpose flour as necessary to prevent the dough from sticking, until the dough is smooth and pliable, about 5 minutes.

5. Spray a 9-by-5-inch loaf pan with the nonstick baking spray. Form the dough into a loaf, and put it into the pan. The short ends of the dough should touch the short ends of the pan.

6. Place the pan in a 5-quart slow cooker. Cover and cook on high for 2 to 2½ hours, or until a food thermometer registers 200°F.

7. Remove the pan from the slow cooker, and let the loaf cool on a wire rack.

Prep It Right

To form dough into a loaf, roll or pat it into an 8-by-9-inch rectangle. Starting with the 8-inch side, roll up the dough tightly. Pinch the seams to seal, and turn the loaf over, seam-side down. Put it into the loaf pan, making sure that the ends touch the pan so the dough is supported as it rises.

NO-KNEAD BREAD

SERVES: 8 • PREP TIME: 10 MINUTES, PLUS 18 TO 24 HOURS TO RISE
COOK TIME: 2 TO 3 HOURS ON HIGH

The no-knead method was popularized by baker Jim Lahey a few years ago. When bread is left to rise for a long period of time, it will knead itself on a microscopic level. These doughs are wetter than regular dough, which helps this process happen. Try it!

1½ cups warm water

1½ teaspoons active dry yeast

½ teaspoon salt

1 cup bread flour

1 cup whole-wheat flour

1 cup all-purpose flour

1 tablespoon olive oil

1. In a large bowl, mix the warm water, yeast, salt, bread flour, whole-wheat flour, and all-purpose flour just until a slightly shaggy dough forms.

2. Brush the top of the dough with the olive oil. Cover the bowl with plastic wrap, and set aside for 18 to 24 hours.

3. When you're ready to bake, stir down the dough.

4. Line a 4- or 5-quart slow cooker with parchment paper. There is no need to grease the paper.

5. Form the dough into a rough ball using floured hands, and set it in the center of the parchment paper in the slow cooker.

6. Cover and cook on high for 2 to 3 hours, or until the bread sounds hollow when you tap it with your fingers and the temperature is about 200°F.

7. Use the parchment paper to remove the bread from the slow cooker. Remove the parchment paper, and let the bread cool on a wire rack.

 The Next Day Homemade breads tend to go stale and even develop mold more quickly than commercial breads. If you don't use your bread within a day or two, slice it and freeze it for up to 3 months for later use. You can toast bread right from the freezer for a quick breakfast.

CHEESY MONKEY BREAD

SERVES: 8 • PREP TIME: 15 MINUTES • COOK TIME: 2 TO 3 HOURS ON HIGH

Monkey bread is so named because of the silly way it's served—you put the loaf out, and people pull off pieces of it to eat. This bread is usually made with sugar and cinnamon, but our savory version is good served with pasta.

1. In a small saucepan over low heat, warm the milk until it is 110°F. Remove the pan from the heat, and add the yeast and sugar. Set aside for 10 minutes.

2. In a large bowl, mix well to combine the whole-wheat flour, bread flour, salt, and ¼ cup of Parmesan cheese.

3. Add the yeast mixture and the olive oil to the bowl, and beat until a dough forms, adding more milk or flour as necessary to make a soft dough. Knead the dough in the bowl for about 5 minutes.

4. Roll the dough out on a floured surface into an 8-inch square. Use a serrated knife to cut it into 64 pieces.

5. Spray a 4-quart slow cooker with the nonstick baking spray. Make an aluminum foil sling, put it in the slow cooker, and spray the foil as well.

¾ cup milk, plus more if needed

1 (0.25-ounce) package active dry yeast

1 teaspoon sugar

½ cup whole-wheat flour, plus more if needed

2 cups bread flour

1 teaspoon salt

1 cup grated Parmesan cheese, divided

2 tablespoons olive oil

Nonstick baking spray with flour

½ cup shredded provolone cheese, divided

½ cup shredded Cheddar cheese, divided

6. In a small bowl, dip the dough pieces one at a time into the remaining ¾ cup of Parmesan cheese.

7. Layer the coated dough pieces in the slow cooker, occasionally adding a layer of the provolone and Cheddar cheeses between each layer of dough pieces. End with a layer of cheese.

8. Cover the top of the slow cooker with a layer of 4 paper towels, add the cover, and cook on high for 2 to 3 hours, or until the bread registers 200°F.

9. Use the foil sling to remove the bread from the slow cooker, and cool on a wire rack.

TEX-MEX CORNBREAD

SERVES: 8 • PREP TIME: 20 MINUTES • COOK TIME: 3 TO 4 HOURS ON LOW

Cornbread made in the slow cooker, just like all quick breads made this way, is really moist and tender. Serve it with Split Pea Soup (page 87), Tomato-Veggie Chowder (page 94), Spicy Red Chili (page 117), or Summer Vegetable Chili (page 127).

1. In a large bowl, mix well to combine the cornmeal, flour mix, sugar, baking powder, and baking soda.

2. Stir in the onions, tomatoes, salsa, milk, egg, egg white, butter, chili powder, and salt until just combined.

3. Spray a 5-quart slow cooker with the nonstick baking spray. Put an aluminum foil sling in the slow cooker, and spray that with baking spray as well. Then add the batter, spreading it evenly across the foil.

4. Cover and cook on low for 3 to 4 hours, or until a toothpick inserted in the center of the bread comes out clean.

5. Let cool for 15 minutes, and remove the bread from the slow cooker using the foil sling. Serve warm.

1 cup yellow or white cornmeal

1 cup gluten-free flour mix

2 tablespoons sugar

3 teaspoons baking powder

1 teaspoon baking soda

½ cup Caramelized Onions (page 181) or onions sautéed until golden brown

2 tablespoons minced sun-dried tomatoes

½ cup salsa

½ cup milk

1 egg

1 egg white

¼ cup butter, melted

1 teaspoon chili powder

¼ teaspoon salt

Nonstick baking spray with flour

CHAI QUICK BREAD

SERVES: 8 • PREP TIME: 20 MINUTES • COOK TIME: 3 TO 4 HOURS ON LOW

Chai is a type of tea made with tea leaves, sugar, milk, and cardamom, which is a spice that comes in pods. Its flavor is delicious in this simple quick bread, and you'll enjoy a mouth watering aroma while it bakes.

½ cup coconut oil

⅓ cup brown sugar

½ cup sugar

2 eggs

½ cup brewed green tea

¼ cup coconut milk

2 teaspoons vanilla

2 cups gluten-free flour mix

1 teaspoon baking powder

¼ teaspoon ground cardamom

⅛ teaspoon salt

Nonstick baking spray with flour

1. In a large bowl, beat to combine the coconut oil, brown sugar, and sugar until fluffy.

2. Beat in the eggs, one at a time.

3. Stir in the green tea, coconut milk, and vanilla, and mix well.

4. Add the flour mix, baking powder, cardamom, and salt, and mix until just combined.

5. Spray a 9-by-5-inch loaf pan with nonstick baking spray, and add the batter.

6. Set the pan in a 5-quart slow cooker.

7. Cover and cook on low for 3 to 4 hours, or until a toothpick inserted into the bread comes out clean.

8. Carefully remove the loaf pan from the slow cooker and let cool for 20 minutes.

9. Remove the bread from the pan and cool completely on a wire rack.

SPICY OLIVE BREAD

SERVES: 8 • PREP TIME: 15 MINUTES • COOK TIME: 3 TO 4 HOURS ON LOW

Olives are delicious—enjoyed by young and old alike. Green olives are picked before they ripen, while black olives ripen on the tree. There are so many different varieties of olives. Use your favorites in this easy recipe—a mix of multiple types is always encouraged.

- 1 ¼ cups all-purpose flour
- ¾ cup whole-wheat flour
- 1 teaspoon baking powder
- ½ teaspoon baking soda
- ¼ teaspoon salt
- ⅛ teaspoon ground cayenne pepper
- 1 teaspoon chili powder
- ⅓ cup extra-virgin olive oil
- 2 eggs, beaten
- ½ cup grated Romano cheese
- 1 cup sour cream
- ⅔ cup chopped pitted olives of your choice
- Nonstick baking spray with flour

1. In a large bowl, mix to combine the all-purpose flour, whole-wheat flour, baking powder, baking soda, salt, cayenne pepper, and chili powder.

2. In a medium bowl, whisk together the olive oil, eggs, cheese, and sour cream.

3. Add the olive oil mixture to the flour mixture, and stir until just combined. Fold in the olives.

4. Spray a 9-by-5-inch loaf pan with the nonstick baking spray, and add the batter.

5. Set the pan in a 5-quart slow cooker.

6. Cover and cook on low for 3 to 4 hours, or until a toothpick inserted into the bread comes out clean.

7. Carefully remove the loaf pan from the slow cooker and let cool for 20 minutes.

8. Remove the bread from the pan and cool completely on a wire rack.

TIRAMISU BREAD

SERVES: 8 TO 10 • PREP TIME: 25 MINUTES • COOK TIME: 3 TO 4 HOURS ON LOW

Tiramisu is an Italian dessert made with ladyfingers soaked in coffee liqueur, then layered with espresso-flavored cream and cocoa powder. I've transformed this dessert into a wonderful breakfast recipe.

⅓ cup butter, melted

½ cup brown sugar

¼ cup sugar

2 eggs

1 cup mascarpone cheese

⅓ cup brewed coffee

3 tablespoons coffee liqueur

2 teaspoons vanilla

2 cups all-purpose flour

1 teaspoon baking powder

⅛ teaspoon salt

2 tablespoons cocoa powder

1 teaspoon instant espresso powder

Nonstick baking spray with flour

½ cup crushed chocolate biscotti crumbs

1. In a large bowl, beat the butter, brown sugar, and sugar until well combined.

2. Beat in the eggs, one at a time.

3. Stir in the mascarpone cheese, coffee, coffee liqueur, and vanilla, and mix well.

4. Add the flour, baking powder, and salt, and mix until just combined.

5. Remove 1 cup of the batter to another small bowl, and stir in the cocoa powder and espresso powder.

6. Spray a 9-by-5-inch loaf pan with nonstick baking spray, and add the plain batter to the slow cooker. Drop the chocolate batter in spoonfuls over the plain batter, and marble them together with a knife. Sprinkle the top of the batter with the crushed cookies.

7. Set the pan into a 5-quart slow cooker.

8. Cover and cook on low for 3 to 4 hours, or until a toothpick inserted into the bread comes out clean.

9. Carefully remove the loaf pan from the slow cooker and let cool for 20 minutes.

10. Remove the bread from the pan, and cool completely on a wire rack.

DESSERTS

STONE FRUIT CRUMBLE

SERVES: 8 • PREP TIME: 25 MINUTES • COOK TIME: 3 TO 3 ½ HOURS ON LOW

Stone fruits include peaches, apricots, nectarines, and plums—basically, anything that has a pit in it. They all combine in this easy recipe that tastes like summer. Pick your own fruit or get the fruit from your favorite stall at the farmers' market.

1. Peel the peaches, cut them in half, and remove the pits. Cut the peaches into large chunks.

2. Cut the plums, apricots, and nectarines in half and remove the pits; they do not need to be peeled. Cut into large chunks.

3. In a 4-quart slow cooker, gently stir to coat the fruit with the lemon juice, sugar, and almond flour.

4. In a large bowl, mix to combine the brown sugar, oatmeal, coconut flour, cashews, baking powder, butter, nutmeg, and salt until crumbly. Spread the mixture over the fruit in the slow cooker.

5. Cover and cook on low for 3 to 3 ½ hours, or until the fruit is tender, and serve.

- 5 peaches
- 5 plums
- 4 apricots
- 4 nectarines
- 2 tablespoons freshly squeezed lemon juice
- ½ cup sugar
- ¼ cup almond flour
- 1 cup brown sugar
- 1 ½ cups old-fashioned oatmeal
- ½ cup coconut flour
- ½ cup chopped cashews
- 1 teaspoon baking powder
- 6 tablespoons butter, melted
- ¼ teaspoon ground nutmeg
- ⅛ teaspoon salt

SALTED CARAMEL BREAD PUDDING

SERVES: 8 • PREP TIME: 15 MINUTES • COOK TIME: 3 TO 4 HOURS ON LOW

....

Bread pudding is the perfect slow cooker recipe. The bread is mixed with eggs, milk, and sugar and cooked until soft and puffy, with browned and crisp edges. Salted Almond-Caramel Sauce makes this recipe very decadent and delicious.

1. In a 4-quart slow cooker, layer the bread cubes and 1 cup of Salted Almond-Caramel Sauce.

2. In a large bowl, beat well to combine the cream, milk, apple juice, sugar, brown sugar, eggs, vanilla, and salt. Pour the mixture over the bread.

3. Cover and cook on low for 3 to 4 hours, or until the bread mixture is puffy and browned around the edges and a food thermometer registers 160°F.

4. Serve the bread pudding warm with the remaining ½ cup of caramel sauce.

1 large loaf ciabatta bread, cubed

1 ½ cups Salted Almond-Caramel Sauce (page 75), divided

1 cup light cream

½ cup whole milk

⅓ cup apple juice

⅓ cup sugar

⅓ cup brown sugar

4 eggs, beaten

4 teaspoons vanilla

½ teaspoon salt

Substitute Tip

If you haven't made the Salted Almond-Caramel Sauce—and I definitely encourage you to make it—you can buy salted caramel sauce in most large grocery stores or online.

SPICED BAKED APPLES

SERVES: 8 • PREP TIME: 25 MINUTES • COOK TIME: 5 TO 7 HOURS ON LOW

Apples stuffed with lots of chewy dried fruit and slowly cooked become tender and sweet with a wonderful texture. It's a great post-Halloween trick-or-treating dessert, keeping the kids from overloading on candy.

1. Peel about an inch around the top of each apple. Carefully cut out the core, starting from the top; do not cut all the way through the apple.

2. Sprinkle the peeled part of the apples and the core with the lemon juice.

3. In a medium bowl, mix well to combine the brown sugar, raisins, cherries, cinnamon, nutmeg, cardamom, curry powder, and salt.

4. Stuff the mixture into the apples, heaping it up slightly as the filling will sink as the apples cook.

5. Place the apples in a 4- or 5-quart slow cooker.

6. Pour the apple juice around the apples but not on top of them.

7. Cover and cook on low for 5 to 7 hours, or until the apples are very tender, and serve.

8 Granny Smith apples

3 tablespoons freshly squeezed lemon juice

1 cup brown sugar

¼ cup golden raisins

¼ cup dried cherries

1 ½ teaspoons ground cinnamon

¼ teaspoon ground nutmeg

⅛ teaspoon ground cardamom

⅛ teaspoon curry powder

⅛ teaspoon salt

¾ cup apple juice

Perfect Pair

This is another wonderful recipe to serve with ice cream. Or whip some heavy (whipping) cream with powdered sugar, and top each apple with a fluffy dollop.

BERRY COBBLER

SERVES: 8 • PREP TIME: 20 MINUTES • COOK TIME: 5 TO 7 HOURS ON LOW

A cobbler is fruit with a batter baked on top. You can use any combination of berries—and whatever proportions—you like in this sweet and tart dessert. Serve it à la mode or with a dollop of whipped cream on top.

1. In a 4- or 5-quart slow cooker, sprinkle the strawberries, blueberries, blackberries, and raspberries with the lemon juice, sugar, and 1/4 cup of almond flour; toss gently to coat.

2. In a large bowl, mix to combine the remaining 2 cups of almond flour with the coconut flour, brown sugar, baking powder, and almonds.

3. Add the coconut oil, apple juice, cinnamon, nutmeg, and salt to the bowl, and mix just until a batter forms. Do not overmix. Pour the batter over the fruit in the slow cooker.

4. Cover and cook on low for 5 to 7 hours, or until the batter is puffy and set, and serve.

3 cups sliced strawberries

3 cups blueberries

2 cups blackberries

2 cups raspberries

2 tablespoons freshly squeezed lemon juice

1/3 cup sugar

2 1/4 cups almond flour, divided

1 cup coconut flour

1/2 cup brown sugar

1 teaspoon baking powder

1/2 cup slivered almonds

1/3 cup melted coconut oil

2/3 cup apple juice

1 1/2 teaspoons ground cinnamon

1/4 teaspoon ground nutmeg

1/8 teaspoon salt

FRUIT and RICE PUDDING

SERVES: 8 • PREP TIME: 15 MINUTES • COOK TIME: 5 TO 6 ½ HOURS ON LOW

Rice pudding is classic comfort food. Typically made with just rice, milk, and sugar, it's good—arguably great—but add dried fruits to bump it up to the next level. The dried fruit also adds an unexpected and welcome texture to the pudding.

1. In a 4-quart slow cooker, stir gently to combine the rice, coconut milk, apple juice, pear nectar, sugar, salt, coconut oil, cherries, golden raisins, currants, and dark raisins.

2. Cover and cook on low for 5 to 6 ½ hours, or until the rice is very tender.

3. Stir in the vanilla.

4. Serve warm or chill in a covered container for a few hours first.

1 cup long-grain rice

4 cups coconut milk

3 cups apple juice

1 cup pear nectar

⅔ cup sugar

⅛ teaspoon salt

2 tablespoons coconut oil

⅓ cup dried cherries

⅓ cup golden raisins

⅓ cup dried currants

½ cup dark raisins

2 teaspoons vanilla

Substitute Tip
You can make this pudding using long-grain brown rice in place of the white rice. The cooking time will be longer, 6 to 7 hours, and the pudding won't be as creamy. But it will be healthier and just as tasty.

CHOCOLATE-PEANUT BUTTER CAKE

SERVES: 8 • PREP TIME: 20 MINUTES • COOK TIME: 5 HOURS ON LOW

Adding peanut butter to chocolate intensifies the chocolate flavor and adds a mellow roundness. If peanuts are a no-no in your house, try making this with almond butter instead. Both versions are amazing and quickly become fan favorites.

1. In a large bowl, mix to combine the flour, sugar, brown sugar, cocoa, baking powder, baking soda, and salt.

2. In a medium bowl, beat well to combine the oil, water, peanut butter, eggs, and vanilla. Stir this mixture into the dry ingredients.

3. Fold in the chocolate chips.

4. Spray a 4-quart slow cooker with the nonstick baking spray. Pour the batter into the slow cooker.

5. Cover and cook on low for 5 hours, or until the cake is just set on top.

6. Turn off the slow cooker and let stand for 10 to 15 minutes before serving.

2 cups all-purpose flour

1 cup sugar

⅔ cup brown sugar

⅔ cup cocoa powder

1½ teaspoons baking powder

½ teaspoon baking soda

¼ teaspoon salt

1 cup vegetable oil

1 cup water

1 cup peanut butter

4 eggs, beaten

2 teaspoons vanilla

1 cup milk chocolate chips

Nonstick baking spray with flour

The Next Day

Leftovers of this cake make wonderful mini trifles. Layer cubes of the cake in individual goblets with fruit jam, whipped cream, and some rum or brandy if you'd like.

PUMPKIN BREAD PUDDING

SERVES: 8 • PREP TIME: 25 MINUTES • COOK TIME: 4 TO 6 HOURS ON LOW

It's all about pumpkin in this bread pudding—pumpkin bread, puréed pumpkin, and pumpkin butter. Serve it for Thanksgiving for an excellent dessert and a nice change from pumpkin pie.

1. Add the Pumpkin-Nut Bread, French bread, and dried cranberries to a 4-quart slow cooker.

2. In a large bowl, stir to combine the pumpkin purée with the cream until smooth. Add the coconut milk, and stir until smooth.

3. Stir in the pumpkin butter, brown sugar, eggs, egg yolks, butter, cinnamon, nutmeg, and salt, and mix well and until smooth. Pour the mixture into the slow cooker.

4. Cover and cook on low for 4 to 6 hours, or until a food thermometer registers 160°F.

5. Serve the pudding with the Salted Almond-Caramel Sauce and, if you like, ice cream.

1 loaf Pumpkin-Nut Bread (page 230), cubed

2 cups cubed French bread

1 cup dried cranberries

1 cup canned solid-pack pumpkin purée (not pumpkin pie filling)

½ cup heavy (whipping) cream

½ cup coconut milk

¼ cup pumpkin butter

½ cup brown sugar

2 eggs

2 egg yolks

⅓ cup butter, melted

2 teaspoons ground cinnamon

⅛ teaspoon ground nutmeg

⅛ teaspoon salt

1 cup Salted Almond-Caramel Sauce (page 75)

MINI CHOCOLATE CHEESECAKES

SERVES: 8 • PREP TIME: 25 MINUTES • COOK TIME: 3 TO 4 HOURS ON LOW

Did you know that you can make individual-size desserts in the slow cooker? All you need are some heatproof custard cups, jars, or ramekins that fit inside the appliance. If eight cups don't fit in your slow cooker, refrigerate some of the batter in the bowl and cook the others later.

1. In a large bowl, beat the cream cheese until soft and fluffy.

2. Gradually beat in the brown sugar and granulated sugar. Beat in the egg and egg yolks.

3. Stir in the melted chocolate chips, espresso powder, cocoa powder, vanilla, and salt.

4. Divide this mixture among eight 4- to 6-ounce heatproof custard cups.

5. Place the cups in a 4- or 5-quart slow cooker. Pour the water into the slow cooker around (not into or over) the little cheesecakes.

6. Cover and cook on low for 3 to 4 hours, or until the cheesecakes are firm.

7. Carefully remove from the slow cooker, and cool on a wire rack for 30 minutes.

8. Refrigerate until cold, and serve.

2 (8-ounce) packages cream cheese, at room temperature

⅓ cup brown sugar

¼ cup granulated sugar

1 egg

2 egg yolks

1 cup semisweet chocolate chips, melted

2 teaspoons espresso powder

3 tablespoons cocoa powder

2 teaspoons vanilla

⅛ teaspoon salt

1 cup water

Perfect Pair

Whip 1 cup heavy (whipping) cream with 2 tablespoons powdered sugar, 2 tablespoons cocoa powder, and 1 teaspoon vanilla for a delicious chocolate topping.

APPLE-PEAR CRISP

SERVES: 8 • PREP TIME: 25 MINUTES • COOK TIME: 4 HOURS ON LOW

Apple crisp is one of the best dessert recipes for fall—and a wonderful excuse to go apple picking. Here we add pears and some crushed graham crackers in the topping for a wonderful treat that will make your home smell incredible.

1. In a 4- or 5-quart slow cooker, toss gently to coat the apples and pears in the lemon juice.

2. Sprinkle the fruit with the sugar and ¼ cup of the almond flour, and toss again.

3. In a large bowl, mix to combine the remaining 2 cups of almond flour with the brown sugar, melted butter, oatmeal, graham cracker crumbs, almonds, cinnamon, cardamom, and salt until crumbly.

4. Spread the crumbly mixture on top of the fruit.

5. Cover and cook on low for 4 hours, or until the fruit is tender.

6. Turn off the slow cooker and let stand for another hour before serving.

12 Granny Smith apples, peeled, cored, and sliced

6 firm pears, peeled, cored, and sliced

2 tablespoons freshly squeezed lemon juice

¾ cup sugar

2¼ cups almond flour, divided

1¼ cups brown sugar

1¼ cups butter, melted

2 cups old-fashioned oatmeal

1 cup coarsely crushed graham cracker crumbs

1 cup chopped almonds

1 teaspoon ground cinnamon

⅛ teaspoon ground cardamom

¼ teaspoon salt

Perfect Pair

This dessert *must* be served with vanilla ice cream, whether you use a dairy or vegan version. The way the ice cream melts into the hot, crumbly topping is simply irresistible.

BROWNIE CAKE

SERVES: 8 • PREP TIME: 15 MINUTES
COOK TIME: 3 TO 4 HOURS ON LOW, PLUS 5 MINUTES ON THE STOVE TOP

This recipe is a cross between a brownie and a cake. It is rich, fudgy, and simply perfect topped with ice cream and caramel sauce. This recipe is perfect for when everyone needs a warm, comforting chocolate fix.

- ¾ cup coconut flour
- ¾ cup almond flour
- ⅓ cup cocoa powder
- 1 teaspoon baking powder
- ⅛ teaspoon salt
- 10 tablespoons butter
- 1 cup semisweet chocolate chips
- 1 cup brown sugar
- ¼ cup sugar
- 3 eggs
- 1 egg yolk
- 2 teaspoons vanilla
- ½ cup ground white chocolate

1. In a large bowl, mix to combine the coconut flour, almond flour, cocoa powder, baking powder, and salt.

2. In a medium saucepan over low heat, melt the butter with the chocolate chips, stirring frequently so the chocolate doesn't burn and the butter and chocolate combine until smooth.

3. Beat the brown sugar and sugar into the chocolate mixture. Add the eggs and egg yolk, one at a time, beating quickly so the eggs don't scramble. Then stir in the vanilla.

4. Stir the chocolate mixture into the flour mixture just until smooth. Stir in the white chocolate.

5. Spoon the batter into a 4- or 5-quart slow cooker, and spread it evenly across the surface.

6. Cover and cook on low for 3 to 4 hours, or until the brownie is set on top.

7. Scoop it out of the slow cooker and serve.

APPLE BROWN BETTY

SERVES: 8 • PREP TIME: 25 MINUTES • COOK TIME: 4 TO 5 HOURS ON LOW

Brown Betty is an old-fashioned recipe made by topping fruit with bread crumbs, and then baking until the fruit is tender and the topping is crisp. This slow cooker recipe recreates those flavors into a beautiful, modern dessert.

1. In a 4- or 5-quart slow cooker, combine the apples, raisins, and lemon juice. Sprinkle with the brown sugar, and mix gently.

2. In a large bowl, combine the bread cubes, sugar, cinnamon, nutmeg, cardamom, and salt. Drizzle with the melted butter, and toss to coat.

3. Put the bread mixture on top of the apples.

4. Cover and cook on low for 4 to 5 hours, or until the apples are tender, and serve.

Substitute Tip

You can make this recipe with pears or peaches, too. Those fruits will have a shorter cooking time because they are softer, so check the food at about 4 hours.

6 apples, peeled, cored, and sliced

1 cup dark raisins

2 tablespoons freshly squeezed lemon juice

½ cup brown sugar

8 slices cinnamon raisin bread, cubed

8 slices French bread, cubed

½ cup sugar

1 teaspoon ground cinnamon

¼ teaspoon ground nutmeg

⅛ teaspoon ground cardamom

⅛ teaspoon salt

½ cup butter, melted

DATE *and* NUT PUDDING

SERVES: 8 • PREP TIME: 20 MINUTES • COOK TIME: 4 TO 5 HOURS ON LOW

Date pudding has been around for hundreds of years, and it is hearty and comforting. In England, it's known as sticky toffee pudding. It's made from dates and chopped pecans and baked in an eggy mixture scented with vanilla. Serve it warm with ice cream.

1. In a large bowl, mix the dates, pecans, brown sugar, almond flour, baking powder, eggs, egg yolk, cream, orange juice, butter, vanilla, and salt until just combined.

2. Pour into a 5-quart slow cooker.

3. Cover and cook on low for 4 to 5 hours, or until a toothpick inserted in the center comes out with just a few crumbs attached to it.

4. Turn off the slow cooker to let cool for 20 minutes, and then serve.

1½ cups chopped pitted dates

1½ cups chopped pecans

1 cup brown sugar

1 cup almond flour

1 teaspoon baking powder

2 eggs

1 egg yolk

⅓ cup heavy (whipping) cream

2 tablespoons freshly squeezed orange juice

6 tablespoons butter, melted

2 teaspoons vanilla

⅛ teaspoon salt

Perfect Pair Hard sauce is the perfect accompaniment to this recipe. Beat ½ cup room temperature butter with 1½ cups powdered sugar, a pinch of salt, 2 teaspoons vanilla, and 2 tablespoons rum (the rum is optional, of course). This firm mixture melts on the warm pudding, making a sauce.

LEMON-ORANGE PUDDING CAKE

SERVES: 8 • PREP TIME: 25 MINUTES • COOK TIME: 4 TO 5 HOURS ON LOW

Pudding cakes are made by making a batter, and then liquid is poured on top. During baking, a cake forms on top, with a pudding-like sauce underneath. The slow cooker is the perfect appliance for this type of recipe because the cake stays moist and tender.

1. In a large bowl, mix to combine the flour, sugar, baking powder, baking soda, salt, lemon peel, and orange peel.

2. Add ½ cup of melted butter, the milk, sour cream, and eggs, and mix well.

3. Spoon the batter into a 4- or 5-quart slow cooker, and top with the oranges.

4. In a medium bowl, mix together the orange juice, lemon juice, orange marmalade, and the remaining 3 tablespoons of melted butter. Pour this mixture over the cake batter in the slow cooker.

5. Cover and cook on low for 4 to 5 hours, or until the cake just springs back when lightly touched with a finger.

6. Serve warm.

2 cups all-purpose flour

¾ cup sugar

2 teaspoons baking powder

1 teaspoon baking soda

¼ teaspoon salt

1 teaspoon grated lemon peel

1 teaspoon grated orange peel

½ cup plus 3 tablespoons butter, melted, divided

½ cup milk

½ cup sour cream

2 eggs

2 (15-ounce) cans mandarin oranges, drained

1 cup freshly squeezed orange juice

⅓ cup freshly squeezed lemon juice

⅓ cup orange marmalade

POACHED PEARS *with* BLUEBERRY SAUCE

SERVES: 8 • PREP TIME: 15 MINUTES • COOK TIME: 3 TO 4 HOURS ON LOW

The slow cooker poaches pears to perfection, making them very tender and sweet. The blueberry sauce is the perfect complement to this simple dessert and a lovely color contrast.

8 ripe but firm Anjou or Bartlett pears

2 tablespoons freshly squeezed lemon juice

1 cup pear nectar

1 cup blueberry jam, divided

2 tablespoons honey

1 teaspoon ground cinnamon

1. Halve the pears lengthwise, being careful to leave the stem attached to one of the halves. Remove the core using a melon baller or a small serrated spoon. Sprinkle the pears with the lemon juice.

2. Place the pears cut-side up in a 4- or 5-quart slow cooker.

3. In a small bowl, mix to combine the pear nectar, 2 tablespoons of blueberry jam, and honey. Pour the mixture around the pears, and sprinkle with the cinnamon.

4. Cover and cook on low for 3 to 4 hours, or until the pears are very tender.

5. Carefully remove the pears from the slow cooker using a slotted spoon, and place them in a serving dish. Spoon some of the cooking liquid over the pears.

6. In a small bowl, mix the remaining blueberry jam with 2 tablespoons of the cooking liquid, and serve with the pears.

Ingredient Tip The best pears for baking are Anjou and Bartlett. Both are available in the fall. Bartlett pears can be found in the typical yellow-green color or in a red variety.

SALTED CARAMEL CHEESECAKE

SERVES: 6 • PREP TIME: 20 MINUTES • COOK TIME: 4 HOURS ON LOW

Salted caramel added to cheesecake elevates this recipe to something you'd buy from a fancy bakery. The pretzel base adds a bit of salty crunch and a toasted flavor. Enjoy this cheesecake with a cup of coffee with more Salted Almond-Caramel Sauce drizzled over the top.

Nonstick baking spray with flour

1 cup pretzel crumbs

3 tablespoons butter, melted

2 (8-ounce) packages cream cheese, at room temperature

½ cup Salted Almond-Caramel Sauce (page 75)

½ cup brown sugar

1 egg

2 egg yolks

2 teaspoons vanilla

Pinch salt

½ cup water

1. Wrap a 6-inch springform pan in two layers of heavy-duty aluminum foil, and spray with nonstick baking spray.

2. In a small bowl, mix to combine the pretzel crumbs with the melted butter. Press the mixture into the bottom of the prepared pan.

3. In a medium bowl, beat to combine the cream cheese, Salted Almond-Caramel sauce, and brown sugar until fluffy. Beat in the egg and egg yolks until smooth, and stir in the vanilla and salt.

4. Spoon the batter into the prepared pan, and smooth the top with the back of a spoon. Place the pan in a 5-quart slow cooker. Add the water to the bottom of the slow cooker, to surround the pan with a water bath.

5. Cover and cook on low for 4 hours.

6. Turn off the slow cooker, and let it stand for 1 hour.

7. Remove the pan from the slow cooker, and let the cheesecake cool for 30 minutes. Then chill it, covered, for 6 to 8 hours before serving.

MARBLE CHEESECAKE

SERVES: 6 • PREP TIME: 25 MINUTES • COOK TIME: 4 HOURS ON LOW, PLUS 5 MINUTES ON THE STOVE TOP

One of the reasons that cheesecakes crack on top when baked in the oven is the dry heat. Baking your cheesecake in the slow cooker eliminates that problem. The top will stay beautifully smooth. This cheesecake is velvety smooth and soft.

1. Wrap a 6-inch springform pan in two layers of heavy-duty aluminum foil. Spray with the nonstick baking spray.

2. In a small bowl, mix to combine the cookie crumbs with the melted butter. Press the mixture into the bottom of the prepared pan.

3. In a medium bowl, beat to combine the cream cheese, mascarpone cheese, and sugar until fluffy. Beat in the egg and egg yolks until smooth, and then stir in the vanilla and salt.

4. Put 1 cup of this batter into a small bowl, and stir in the melted semisweet chocolate chips until blended and smooth.

5. Pour the plain cream cheese mixture into the prepared pan. Spoon the chocolate mixture onto the plain batter using a tablespoon. Marble the two mixtures together using a toothpick.

Nonstick baking spray with flour

1 cup chocolate cookie crumbs

3 tablespoons butter, melted

2 (8-ounce) packages cream cheese, at room temperature

½ cup mascarpone cheese

⅔ cup sugar

1 egg

2 egg yolks

2 teaspoons vanilla

Pinch salt

½ cup semisweet chocolate chips, melted

½ cup water

1 cup milk chocolate chips

2 tablespoons heavy (whipping) cream

6. Set the pan in a 5-quart slow cooker. Add the water to the bottom of the slow cooker so the pan is surrounded by a bath.

7. Cover and cook on low for 4 hours. Turn off the slow cooker, and let it stand for 1 hour.

8. Remove the pan from the slow cooker, and let the cheesecake cool for 30 minutes.

9. In a small saucepan over low heat, melt the milk chocolate chips with the cream, stirring frequently so the chocolate doesn't burn and it combines with the cream until smooth; drizzle the mixture over the cheesecake.

10. Chill the cheesecake for 4 to 6 hours before serving.

COCONUT-PEAR RICE PUDDING

SERVES: 8 • PREP TIME: 15 MINUTES • COOK TIME: 5 TO 6 HOURS ON LOW

With most rice pudding recipes, you cook the rice first. With this recipe, the rice cooks right in the slow cooker, so it's less labor intensive to make. Ah, the beauty of the slow cooker.

1. In a 4- or 5-quart slow cooker, stir well to combine the rice, coconut milk, pear nectar, sugar, coconut, pears, coconut oil, and salt.

2. Cover and cook on low for 5 to 6 hours, or until the rice is very tender. Transfer the pudding to a large bowl and let cool.

3. In a small bowl, beat the cream with the powdered sugar and vanilla until stiff. Fold the cream mixture into the pudding.

4. Cover and chill for 3 to 4 hours before serving.

The Next Day Use this leftover rice pudding to make little tartlets. Buy purchased graham cracker tartlet shells, and spoon rice pudding into them. Top with whipped cream and serve.

1¼ cups long-grain white rice

2 cups coconut milk

2 cups pear nectar

¾ cup sugar

¾ cup shredded coconut

2 pears, peeled, cored, and cubed

3 tablespoons coconut oil

⅛ teaspoon salt

¾ cup heavy (whipping) cream

1 tablespoon powdered sugar

2 teaspoons vanilla

POACHED FIGS

SERVES: 8 • PREP TIME: 15 MINUTES • COOK TIME: 5 TO 6 HOURS ON LOW

Dried figs can be purchased year round, unlike fresh figs, which are in season in early June and then again in the early fall. They become soft and tender when poached for a long time in the slow cooker.

3 cups pear nectar or white wine

1 cup sugar

⅓ cup honey

24 dried figs

2 teaspoons grated orange peel

Pinch salt

1. In a 4-quart slow cooker, stir to combine the nectar, sugar, and honey. Add the figs, orange peel, and salt, and gently stir.

2. Cover and cook on low for 5 to 6 hours, or until the figs are very tender.

3. Spoon the figs into a serving dish with some of the cooking syrup, and serve.

Substitute Tip You can cook any dried fruit this way, from dried apricots and prunes to dried apples and mangoes.

CRÈME CARAMEL

SERVES: 6 • PREP TIME: 15 MINUTES • COOK TIME: 4 TO 5 HOURS ON LOW

Crème Caramel is a smooth and velvety vanilla custard topped with a crunchy broiled sugar mixture. The slow cooker is a great appliance to make this recipe in, since the moist heat helps keep the custard soft. There's nothing quite as satisfying as tapping your spoon on the hard sugar surface.

6 egg yolks

⅓ cup granulated sugar

2 tablespoons powdered sugar

2 cups heavy (whipping) cream

1 vanilla bean

1 teaspoon vanilla extract

Pinch salt

Unsalted butter, at room temperature

1½ cups water

⅓ cup brown sugar

1. In a large mixing bowl, beat the egg yolks, granulated sugar, and powdered sugar until the mixture is light yellow.

2. Stir in the cream.

3. Cut open the vanilla bean lengthwise, and scrape out the seeds. Add the seeds to the custard mixture along with the vanilla extract and salt, and stir well.

4. Grease a 1-quart glass baking dish with the butter. Add the custard to the dish, and place the dish in a 4- or 5-quart slow cooker.

5. Pour the water into the slow cooker, being careful not to get any in the custard.

6. Cover and cook on low for 4 to 5 hours, or until the custard is set but still a little soft in the middle.

7. Remove the pan from the slow cooker, and chill in the refrigerator for 5 to 6 hours.

8. When you're ready to eat, sprinkle the brown sugar evenly over the custard. Place it under a preheated broiler until the sugar melts, or use a small torch to melt the sugar. Serve immediately.

BUTTERSCOTCH-CHOCOLATE FONDUE

SERVES: 8 • PREP TIME: 15 MINUTES • COOK TIME: 2 TO 3 HOURS ON LOW

Fondue is a fun recipe to make for entertaining. Everyone gathers around the table and spears cookies, fruit chunks, and pieces of cake to dip into the rich sauce.

1. In an 8-cup bowl that will fit inside a 4- or 5-quart slow cooker, stir well to combine the butter, brown sugar, cocoa powder, chocolate chips, condensed milk, honey, butterscotch sauce, vanilla, and salt.

2. Put the bowl into the slow cooker, and add the water to the bottom of the slow cooker, creating a bath around the bowl.

3. Cover and cook on low for 2 to 3 hours, stirring the mixture occasionally, until the sauce is smooth.

4. Serve with cake cubes, fresh fruit pieces, waffle sticks, or sugar cookies for dipping.

½ cup butter

2 cups brown sugar

⅓ cup cocoa powder

1 cup semisweet chocolate chips

1 (14-ounce) can sweetened condensed milk

½ cup honey

½ cup butterscotch ice cream sauce

2 teaspoons vanilla

⅛ teaspoon salt

½ cup water

10 TIPS FOR CLEANING YOUR SLOW COOKER

1 The ceramic insert can usually be cleaned after a brief soak in warm water and a bit of dish soap. Always remove the insert from the metal surround and make sure it is completely cool before you starting cleaning.

2 Baking soda makes a good scouring powder to clean stubborn or stuck-on foods. Sprinkle some on the damp ceramic insert and scrub with a plastic "scrubbie."

3 Never use a metal scouring pad on the ceramic insert, or you may scratch the surface. Food can collect in the scratches and become a source for bacterial growth.

4 Many ceramic inserts are dishwasher-safe. Read the booklet that came with your slow cooker to make sure the insert can be cleaned this way. Put the insert on the top shelf of the dishwasher.

5 For really stubborn stains on the ceramic insert, try using denture cleaner. Drop it into the insert that has been filled with cool water, cover, and let stand for a few hours, then clean with a plastic scrubbie and soap.

6 You can also fill the slow cooker insert almost to the top with water, then add ½ cup of vinegar and ½ cup baking soda (add the soda very slowly, about a tablespoon at a time). Cover and let stand for a few hours, then empty the insert and wash with soap and water.

7 If all else fails, put some dish soap and baking soda into the ceramic insert. Fill it with water, then place the insert into the metal surround. Cover the slow cooker and put it on low for 3 to 4 hours. Unplug the appliance, let it cool, then empty the insert and wash.

8 The metal surround should be cleaned only with a damp cloth and some mild soap, and only it is unplugged and has completely cooled.

9 If there are any stains on the inside of the metal surround, you can use a paste of baking soda and water. Scrub gently using a plastic scrubbie; never use a metal scouring pad.

10 Use a slow cooker-approved plastic cooking bag, line the slow cooker insert with aluminum foil or parchment paper, or spray it thoroughly with nonstick cooking spray before you add the food.

MEASUREMENT CONVERSIONS

VOLUME EQUIVALENTS (LIQUID)

US STANDARD	US STANDARD (OUNCES)	METRIC (APPROXIMATE)
2 tablespoons	1 fl. oz.	30 mL
¼ cup	2 fl. oz.	60 mL
½ cup	4 fl. oz.	120 mL
1 cup	8 fl. oz.	240 mL
1½ cups	12 fl. oz.	355 mL
2 cups or 1 pint	16 fl. oz.	475 mL
4 cups or 1 quart	32 fl. oz.	1 L
1 gallon	128 fl. oz.	4 L

OVEN TEMPERATURES

FAHRENHEIT (F)	CELSIUS (C) (APPROXIMATE)
250°	120°
300°	150°
325°	165°
350°	180°
375°	190°
400°	200°
425°	220°
450°	230°

VOLUME EQUIVALENTS (DRY)

US STANDARD	METRIC (APPROXIMATE)
⅛ teaspoon	0.5 mL
¼ teaspoon	1 mL
½ teaspoon	2 mL
¾ teaspoon	4 mL
1 teaspoon	5 mL
1 tablespoon	15 mL
¼ cup	59 mL
⅓ cup	79 mL
½ cup	118 mL
⅔ cup	156 mL
¾ cup	177 mL
1 cup	235 mL
2 cups or 1 pint	475 mL
3 cups	700 mL
4 cups or 1 quart	1 L

WEIGHT EQUIVALENTS

US STANDARD	METRIC (APPROXIMATE)
½ ounce	15 g
1 ounce	30 g
2 ounces	60 g
4 ounces	115 g
8 ounces	225 g
12 ounces	340 g
16 ounces or 1 pound	455 g

REFERENCES

Gunnars, Kris. "Ten Proven Benefits of Kale." *Authority Nutrition*. Accessed June 8, 2016. https://authoritynutrition.com/10-proven-benefits-of-kale.

Moll, Jennifer. "Chickpeas: Can They Lower Your Cholesterol?" *VeryWell*. March 8, 2016. https://www.verywell.com/chickpeas-lower-cholesterol-697624.

Reynolds. "Reynolds Slow Cooker Liners Frequently Asked Questions." Accessed June 8, 2016. http://www.reynoldskitchens.com/media/171330/scl_faq.pdf.

INDEX

ABOUT THE AUTHOR

Linda Larsen is the author of more than 30 cookbooks, including *The Complete Slow Cooking for Two*, among other slow cooking titles. Linda is also the Busy Cooks Expert on About.com. An omnivore who routinely makes vegetarian meals for family members, Linda brings both her slow cooking expertise and her please-any-crowd recipes to *The Ultimate Vegetarian Slow Cooker*.